Praise for *#SalesTruth*

"Bold. Blunt. Truth. Mike will disrupt your thinking and challenge you with simple sales solutions as only he can. Proceed with caution—powerful insights on every page."

—**MARK HUNTER,**
author of *High-Profit Prospecting*

"It is rare that a book speaks a truth so strongly and so clearly that it defines an era. *#SalesTruth* is that book. Weinberg tells the #SalesTruth in his blunt, inimitable style, delivered with a sense of humor, and heavy on the practical, tactical approach that is his trademark. —**ANTHONY IANNARINO,**
author of *Eat Their Lunch:*
Winning Customers Away from Your Competition

"You likely have never before gasped while reading a sales book, so brace yourself for some real, honest, potentially painful, truths including a debunking of my personal favorite sales myth that 'everything has changed.' You will be a better salesperson and sales leader after implementing these #SalesTruths. Do yourself a favor and read this book now." —**ANDREA WALTZ,**
coauthor of *Go for No!*

"Mike Weinberg takes a blowtorch to the trendy sales 'shiny objects' and fads, most of which are counterproductive to the fundamental sales activities that always have, and always will, produce results. He offers his no-holds-barred, back-to-reality framework on exactly what TO DO to crush it in sales and prospecting. Entertaining and educational, this book should be part of every salesperson's toolbox." —**ART SOBCZAK,**
author of *Smart Calling,*
host of *The Art of Sales* podcast

"Mike Weinberg has done it again. He obliterates all of the latest shiny sales shortcuts and reorients us toward real selling and real results. *#SalesTruth* will leave you motivated and ready to kick butt. Happy hunting!" —**EVAN WALDMAN,**
CEO, Essex Industries

"The #SalesTruth is in this book, and it's on a short list of the most impactful books about professional selling I've ever read. Absolute gems include the 'Bridge Line' in chapter 10 and the 'Money Line' in chapter 11, and the 'Not-So-Extraordinary' keys to success in chapter 15 could alone double your revenue!"

—JEFF BAJOREK,
host of *The Why and the Buy* podcast

"I love this book, and if you or your team are confused or struggling to bring in new business, get *#SalesTruth* now! While I prefer to have Mike in front of our sales team in person, this book is the next best thing to deliver the straightforward, easy-to-implement, powerful advice you need. *#SalesTruth* is now required reading for our managers and will be part of our sales reps' training."

—PAGE NAFTEL,
President, Ram Tool Construction Supply

"Beware the false prophets who proclaim the death of traditional hard work—prospecting, calendar management, listening before pitching! Business owners, sales executives, and salespeople will find *#SalesTruth* to be a pragmatic and practical guide to what works in sales with common sense, hard truths, and direct takeaways that debunk the excuses for poor sales performance. Mike's got great advice and relevant case studies that smart sales reps and their managers will want to implement ASAP."

—GINA HOAGLAND,
Cofounder, Collaborative Strategies, Inc.,
and Chairwoman, Triad Bank

"My friend and long-time sales advisor, Mike Weinberg, delivers a bold, blunt call to action for everyone seeking to grow their business! Just like a great golf swing, mastery of fundamentals has a bigger impact on your success than the hottest trend or technology. Ready to improve your sales game? Read this for a solid reminder of the basics, sales lessons from the 2016 election, and examples that will help you improve from the moment you start reading." —MARK PETERMAN,
CEO, Cornerstone Solutions Group

"If you liked *New Sales. Simplified.* and *Sales Management. Simplified.*, then you will LOVE *#SalesTruth*. Mike Weinberg is practical and to the point, and brings clarity to today's most critical sales issues and challenges. Every sales professional should own this book!"
—JAMES MUIR,
author of *The Perfect Close*

"Buckle up and get ready for an entertaining journey, as Mike Weinberg navigates the tumult created by today's so-called sales experts. In his unique and engaging style, Mike delivers actionable truth you can start using immediately to close more sales."
—JOE TARULLI,
General Manager and Sales Leader, Pyrotek

"The sales faculty at Kansas State University are huge Mike Weinberg fans! Thanks to Mike and his great work, our students know how to prospect, articulate value, and create and close new sales opportunities. *#SalesTruth* delivers even more no-nonsense wisdom and most certainly will be the next reading assignment for K-State sales students. It should be your next reading assignment, too!"
—DAWN DEETER,
Director, National Strategic Selling Institute,
and professor, Kansas State University

"Packed with piercing honesty, Mike Weinberg's *#SalesTruth* is a must-read for winning salespeople who want to win even more! It's not an exaggeration to say that those who read it and live by these proven principles will double their earning potential."
—PENNY QUELLER,
Senior VP and General Manager, Monster Worldwide

"Bold, brilliant, and packed with blunt truth! There's no secret to sales success, and Mike brazenly drills right at the core foundational level, delivering much-needed tough love while laying down the sales gauntlet. Take *#SalesTruth* to heart because Mike poured his heart and soul into every page."
—LARRY LEVINE,
author of *Selling from the Heart*

"Highly funded sales-tool vendors and social-selling experts would love to convince modern sellers that everything has changed in sales. Mike proves conclusively with case studies from his clients across all industries that that's simply not the case. And I love that Mike presents proof that procurement is not omnipotent! #SalesTruth is not for the faint of heart and is the perfect 202 companion to New Sales. Simplified."

—JUSTIN MICHAEL,
VP of Sales, Kochava

"A wonderful reminder that sales is a noble profession and that the most successful sellers have their customer's best interests at heart and are motivated to deliver a valuable outcome that improves the customer's condition! #SalesTruth powerfully captures the challenges created when we chase the 'secret sales sauce' instead of executing the basics that drive results."

—TRACEY CRAIK,
Regional Sales Director, TEC Equipment, Inc.

"Execute the basics, utilize every tool, listen to your customers, and deliver value on time, every time. No one distills the truth about the dignity and hard work of sales professionals—from every walk, industry, and corner of the world—better than Mike Weinberg! He raises the game of both sellers and sales leaders, and delivers #SalesTruth that is helping our team drive results."

—DAN GRANT,
VP of Sales and Business Development, Skyline Champion

"Mike's previous books New Sales. Simplified. and Sales Management. Simplified. improved our team's approach to selling and managing. #SalesTruth continues the trend, providing fabulous content for our sales coaches to have candid conversations around creating opportunities, rather than chasing them!"

—SCOTT COUP,
Director of Commercial Sales, Enterprise Bank & Trust

"Mike is vulnerable and pushes the limits with #SalesTruth. Written in his familiar straightforward and anecdotal style, he debunks myths, speaks honestly, and will convict those who insist on searching for the silver sales bullet."

—TODD HOLCOMBE,
Director of Training, Ram Tool Construction Supply

#SalesTruth

Debunk the Myths.

Apply Powerful Principles.

Win More New Sales.

MIKE WEINBERG

HARPERCOLLINS
LEADERSHIP

AN IMPRINT OF HARPERCOLLINS

Published by HarperCollins Leadership, an imprint of HarperCollins Focus LLC.

Book design by Pauline Neuwirth, Neuwirth & Associates.

ISBN 978-1-5955-5754-4 (eBook)
ISBN 978-1-5955-5722-3 (HC)
ISBN 978-1-4002-1746-5 (ITPE)

Library of Congress Cataloguing-in-Publication Data
Library of Congress Control Number: 2019930197

Printed in the United States of America
19 20 21 22 LSC 10 9 8 7 6 5 4 3 2 1

#SalesTruth is dedicated to the warrior sellers and sales leaders who drive results and create value for their customers, their companies, and themselves.

CONTENTS

CONTENTS

Foreword

There has never been a greater need for a book on the truth about what it takes to succeed in sales. Over the past decade, those of us in sales have been bombarded with a glut of ideas and opinions about sales, much of them coming from people who lack the knowledge and experience to offer sales advice. A good portion of the offered advice was contrarian only to gain attention and to create a dominant narrative: "Everything in sales has changed. And irrevocably."

These contrarian, ill-formed, and ill-conceived opinions argued against reality. In fact, the fundamentals hadn't changed. A practice becomes fundamental through its ability to produce sustained results over time. Fundamentals are what you might also call #SalesTruths.

A few of us found the new experts' words and ideas insufferable. While the rest of the industry acquiesced to the notion that the social tools spelled doom for the fundamentals of effective selling, a small few of us fought to hold back the tide—and the damage it inflicted on salespeople and sales organizations. The new "sales experts'" lies were only exceeded by the number of proponents sharing them. They said things like, "Never cold call again," and "Connect with people on the platforms and engage them there," promising companies more new opportunities without any real effort on the part of the salesperson.

If promises of every sales rep being able to succeed in sales weren't enough to cause sales managers and sales leaders to acquiesce, the new "sales experts" would frighten them into "developing" the "modern salesperson," one who was social and connected, just like the experts they followed. Sales leaders were told that if they weren't training their people to use the new social platforms, their business would be irreparably harmed by their stubborn adherence to "the old ways." They were told that the traditional "sales role" was now irrelevant because buyers were on the internet and had access to all the information they needed, with the salesperson unable to create any real value outside of being a servile errand boy or girl.

One of the few who "stood athwart history yelling stop" is the author of the book you hold in your hands (or are listening to between sales calls or on an airplane en route to see a client). The author of this book is a dear friend and co-conspirator. At the very height of "social selling," he published his first book, *New Sales. Simplified: The Essential Handbook for Prospecting and New Business Development,* a book that implored salespeople to "select targets," "sharpen their sales weapons," and "block time to pick up the phone" to schedule meetings. If these timeless fundamentals of selling weren't so compelling, NSS wouldn't have close to 600 reviews on Amazon.com with the average review being five stars. If Mike Weinberg were incorrect in his advice, he wouldn't be one of the most sought-after speakers and consultants in sales today.

Starving for Truth in a Post-Truth World

To those of us close to him, Mike Weinberg is "the Honey Bad-ger." He is devastatingly blunt, brutally honest, and inexhaustibly determined to tell the truth: #SalesTruth. In this book, Mike shares with you what the new "sales experts" suggest you should do to be successful in sales now, using their own words. The duty to prepare you for what you are going to read falls to me, but I am in some ways inadequate; you are likely to doubt that anyone would dare write anything so ridiculous as what Mike documents here. There isn't a better person to repudiate their poor ideas and "advice," and to do so with a sense of humor that drives home the truth (while making you laugh out loud, and maybe tear up a little).

In the first four chapters, Mike dispels the myths and elimi-nates the lies, all the while providing you an understanding as to why these false ideas exist and the motives of the false teachers. My promise here is that you are going to be outraged by what passes for sales advice and entertained by Mike's assessment.

In part II, Mike provides you with the truth about selling effec-tively now (and deep into the future). If you don't have a step-by-step guide for winning more deals, creating new opportunities, taking back your calendar, and calling your shots by targeting your dream clients, you will have all of this accomplished by the end of chapter 9. If you are not sure how to improve your pros-pecting because you need better messaging, in two succinct and powerful chapters, you will have the confidence to book new meetings without hesitation.

It's hard for me to play favorites, but in a single chapter on selling at a higher price, you will understand more about how to embrace your differentiation and the competitive advantage it provides you. If you want to know what the top 10 percent of salespeople do that place them on that lofty perch at the top of the stack ranking, chapter 15 will give you two case studies that are remarkably unremarkable in that the best reps in the world are the best at the fundamentals.

If you want the truth, unfiltered, unadulterated, and made practical and tactical, you will find just that between the cover of this book. Embrace the truth, follow Mike's advice, and make many more new sales!

Anthony Iannarino,
author of *Eat Their Lunch: Winning
Customers Away from Your Competition*

Acknowledgments

I am beyond blessed by all the support I received during the planning and writing of this book. My first expression of gratitude goes directly to my talented new friend and senior editor at HarperCollins Leadership, Tim Burgard. His excitement about this project and his guidance were invaluable.

No one paid a greater price for this book than Katie, my bride and best friend. She was incredibly gracious as I wrote this manuscript while attempting to juggle my client workload and crazy travel schedule. Huge thanks to my beautiful and patient wife, without whom I'd be lost or worse, and double thanks for her excellent early stage editing and suggestions.

To the three greatest young adult children on Earth—Kurt, Haley, and Corey—thank you for all your encouragement, amusement, and opinions as I dove deep into this project. It is a joy to see each of you thriving; I could not be more proud of you. And deep gratitude to my parents, who still find ways to cheer on and inspire their fifty-one-year-old son. You are loved and appreciated.

To my mastermind group and partners in the OutBound Conference—Jeb Blount, Mark Hunter, and Anthony Iannarino—thank you for your boldness, ideas, inspiration, truth-telling, and transparency. You have made me a better consultant and speaker, and you three are making a huge dent in the sales community at large. To my wise, mature (and aging), dearest friends and advisors—Shane Johnston, Rob Morton, and Mark Peterman—I thank you again for your wisdom and for never letting me settle or get complacent. And to Mary Oliver, who keeps the trains running on the tracks and my head from exploding, thank you for how you care for, support, and protect me. I could not do this without you.

Finally, to my clients who have entrusted me to help create healthy, high-performance sales cultures, effective sales leaders, and drive more New Sales, thank you not only for your confidence but for allowing me to do what I love.

PART I

The #Truth About the "Experts"

CHAPTER 1

Truth, What Is Truth?

I have spent such a ridiculous amount of time on airplanes this past year (often mulling over ideas for this book) that it's only fitting I am writing the first chapter on a flight to South Africa. After a day to recover from this twenty-four-hour journey, I'll be doing what I pretty much do every week—sharing blunt observations with business leaders, executives, sales managers, and salespeople about why they are not winning as many New Sales as they'd like, and then providing simple, practical, powerful fixes to help them create a healthy, high-performance sales culture and close more new business. Said differently, I tell them the truth about sales.

It's an honor and a privilege and seems to have become my calling—speaking #SalesTruth to sales leaders and salespeople.

• • •

Who Are You to Declare What's True?

I get it. It's nervy and could certainly be perceived as self-righteous to declare that you've got the corner on *the truth* about something as big and important as sales. Please hear me on this: I don't have the corner on the truth and would never claim I did. When I observe, consult, or coach an executive or salesperson, or facilitate a workshop or training session, I learn something new Every. Single. Day. That is why I absolutely love what I do. I am always learning, and I get to experience firsthand what is working in sales and sales management, and what is not. Then I get to share those observations with my readers and clients.

Those who know me, read my books and blog, or follow me on Twitter and LinkedIn are keenly aware (and even appreciate) that I simply call it like I see it. Yes, on occasion, I speak and write in extremes to make a point, often in an attempt to deliver a wake-up call, hoping to swing the pendulum back toward the center, and that is *exactly* my hope in writing this book.

The amount of noise and flat-out disinformation about sales and sales management are at an all-time high. It was bad seven years ago, so bad—particularly surrounding prospecting and developing new business—that I was motivated to write my first book, *New Sales. Simplified.* And, amazingly, as hard as it is to believe, the confusion and chaos are even worse today.

There has never been more confusion, frankly, because there have never been more theories and opinions and so many (free) channels to broadcast this disinformation. Self-proclaimed sales "experts" and "thought leaders" have sprung up everywhere— many of whom have amassed significant followings by preaching popular nonsense that tickles the ears of sales leaders and sellers craving an easy-button or magic fix. Point out the stupidity, inaccuracy, and inconsistency of what these "experts" are posting, and they are quick to reply defensively, pointing to the number of "likes" their articles receive. To quote my friend and author of *High-Profit Prospecting*, Mark Hunter, "Salespeople cannot take likes and clicks to the bank." And I have joked that the credibility of many of today's faux sales improvement gurus is inversely proportional to the number of people who "like" their posts. Translation: Popularity does not equate to the helpfulness/usefulness/ effectiveness of the information presented. In fact, it's often quite the opposite.

Everything Has Not Changed

Many of today's nouveau "experts" love to tell us that *everything* has changed. It's a dangerous new world and all the rules have changed, they claim. Nothing that used to work in sales or sales management still works today. *Nothing.* Traditional approaches, techniques, and methodologies are no longer effective. In fact, they proffer that if you dare even try to deploy old-school, traditional methods, you're not just an idiot bound to fail but also a Luddite from the Dark Ages who deserves to be ridiculed. And if you think that I might be exaggerating even a bit here, see the examples in the next chapter.

What's so amusing and so irritating to me is that I see the exact opposite. The. Exact. Opposite.

The most effective executives, sales managers, and salespeople I observe are masters at the basics. They have perfected old-school, traditional approaches. Instead of constantly entertaining themselves by shopping for the latest, greatest, and trendiest new tool, toy, or trick, they stay with the tried-and-true, proven fundamentals of sales and sales leadership. Not sexy, but incredibly effective.

Let me make that point again from a different angle, because I desperately want you to digest this truth: Despite what you hear and read from today's trendiest, self-proclaimed thought leaders, I have *never* seen a salesperson or sales team fail because they lack a recently invented sales tool, or because they had not yet adopted a newly created sales process.

I don't know how to make this next point graciously or without coming across as arrogant, so I am just going to say it in abject frustration because I am so tired of the half-truths and false promises giving false hope to salespeople and managers: You would be hard-pressed to find a sales consultant/trainer/speaker who's been on more airplanes and in more companies than I have the past few years. I have been around the globe helping sales teams in every industry—from mortgages to machinery, from plastics and polymers to payroll services, from defense to distribution, from big data to big trucks, and from SaaS (software as a service) to trash. And I can emphatically and unequivocally state that, regardless of what the so-called experts are writing on LinkedIn or quoting in their "studies," it's not their beloved, newfound tool or process that's missing—it's a solid execution of the basics. They can wax eloquently about their theories, brag about how many people "like" their posts, speak for free at the online virtual sales conferences, and cite supposedly valid research to their hearts' content. I know what I am seeing and hearing with my own eyes and ears: The sales world is desperate for rigor and discipline around the fundamentals, not fancy new tricks.

Almost every week, I speak with leaders of struggling sales organizations who have spent crazy amounts of money and time buying into and then attempting to implement new tools and methods because they (wrongly or sadly) believed that the promised panacea would solve all that ails their sales. Well, the fact that they're calling for help *after* spending (wasting) all those dollars, all that time, and all that energy chasing the shiny new [fill in this month's hot sales topic here] sure says a lot, doesn't it?

Let me make sure you are not reading more into this than I am writing. I am not declaring that you and your sales team don't need tools, processes, or technology. Of course, you do. What I am most definitely stating is that the people winning big in sales today are doing so because they have mastered the basics, and those who are struggling, particularly in the area of developing new business and winning New Sales, are flailing because they are not executing the basics well. Despite loud protestations from many "experts," the flat-out truth is that what has worked exceedingly well in sales and sales management for the past couple decades is still the (not so) secret to sales success today. As crazy as it may sound, if I introduced you to the top-performing salesperson at each of my clients across that eclectic mix of industries listed, you would see these top producers deploying the very same mindset, approaches, behaviors, and disciplines that I observed in top-producing salespeople five years ago, ten years ago, and fifteen years ago. #SalesTruth. The best sellers and the best leaders excel at the fundamentals of their job. They are masters at their craft, because they have mastered the basics.

Before we unpack these critical fundamentals in part II ("The #Truth About Winning More New Sales"), please indulge me a bit further as we take a look at the hypocrisy and nonsense preached by these dangerous, disingenuous "experts" who I believe are actually hurting, not helping, the sales community.

CHAPTER 2

Be Very Wary of the Nouveau Experts and False Teachers

I did not want to write this chapter, but my eyes and my conscience compelled me to. My intention here is not to be meanspirited; it is simply to point out the bizarre inconsistencies between what some modern popular sales "experts" are proclaiming and what anyone who has succeeded in sales for any length of time, has successfully led a sales organization, or has a shred of common sense, knows is true.

The United States Department of Homeland Security, in an effort to keep the public vigilant about terrorism threats, has promoted this expression: *If You See Something, Say Something.* I like that. It's simple. It's catchy. It's easy to remember.

Well, over the past five or so years, colleagues whom I trust and respect in the sales improvement industry and I have been seeing a lot of things causing us to do double takes. Practically every week, my partners in the OutBound Conference (Jeb Blount, Mark Hunter, Anthony Iannarino), and I exchange a handful of group text messages. One of us will read or hear something from an "expert" that is blatantly false, misleading, and often dangerous. We'll pass along the article to one another so we can collectively shake our heads and, for a while, one or more of us would challenge the misinformation publicly—either by publishing our own counterargument in an article, or, by simply posting a comment pointing out the inconsistency and absurdity being offered by the "expert." Simply put, we were *seeing something* that didn't look right and *saying something* to warn others.

The problem, we discovered, is that it's very hard to win an intelligent argument with people untethered to the truth because their livelihood is tied to the agenda they are promoting. Yes, that sounds eerily close to the situation we have politically here in the United States, where there is no longer civil discourse or healthy debate about any hot political topic or candidate. But I'll hold off going further into politics until chapter 4, where, against my better judgment, I am going to share powerful sales lessons from the 2016 US presidential election, because there is a lot of #SalesTruth to be gleaned. Please resist the temptation to jump ahead to see me risk my friendships and business by giving a sales coach's perspective on the shocking election of Donald Trump as president. For now, let's stick with taking on false teaching and misguided sales advice.

The other painful lesson I learned is that it is really, really, really hard to wage a battle online with people who have way too much time on their hands as they sit behind a keyboard and bury you with BS.

Those who are successful in the sales improvement industry are very busy. Beyond busy. We are buried by more opportunities for paying work than we can handle. And contrary to those who want to gauge #SalesTruth (and sales improvement effectiveness) by the number of *likes* they receive, the reality is that, in this business, the true measures of success for sales consultants, coaches, trainers, and speakers are travel, paid engagements, and time spent helping clients.

Watch Out for Sales Fads, Flavors of the Day, and Bandwagon Jumpers

In my previous book—*Sales Management. Simplified.*—I chastised sales leaders for our tendency to chase shiny new toys. As a group, we're a gullible bunch and always looking for an edge. So, when we hear about a new thing—a slick tool, cool new process, or a potential quick fix—our FOMO (fear of missing out) kicks into high gear. We are typically quick to investigate and often too quick to go all in and adopt this new thing/approach/process/tool.

Well, you know whose FOMO is even worse than that of sales managers and salespeople? Yup. Sales improvement gurus! Nothing has been more entertaining in the last decade than watching people who make a living in the sales improvement industry jump on the bandwagon of each hot, trending sales fad and flavor of the day.

First, it was inbound. But at least with inbound, they called it what it was—marketing. Inbound marketing. Unlike the #socialselling-movement leaders who followed, the inbound marketers were not telling salespeople that they'd be better off doing marketing activities rather than sales activities.

Inbound was followed by the rapid rise of social selling, which "borrowed" many of its themes and principles from inbound marketing. This long-lived fad took on a life of its own, and it requires more than just a passing mention here. We will circle back to examine the bold claims many #socialselling "experts" have been preaching, and we will contrast those with what some actually practice to drive their own businesses.

A few years ago, the term sales enablement became trendy and garnered significant momentum, so much so that today we have an entire field of people and positions working under that banner and telling us that it is the future of selling. However, it's a bit confusing since there have been regular attempts to define and redefine sales enablement and there appears to be zero agreement about exactly what it is and what it means. Try googling the term if you're curious—you'll get a myriad of "expert" opinions. And feel free to read articles summarizing the Sales Enablement Society Annual Conference.

I read a great and refreshingly honest post on Membrain .com's blog written by a founding member (one of a hundred founding members) and Dallas Chapter president of the Sales Enablement Society. He summarized the 2017 conference beautifully, and his transparency in reporting the agenda and key takeaways only furthers the point that even the "experts" are not sure what sales enablement is. He jokes that those who tell you they do are likely attempting to sell you something! (See the blog at https://tinyurl.com/y8tgnk5s, where the writer admits, "Ask 10 companies what sales enablement means, and you're likely to get 13 different answers.")

Zackly my point! There's this hot bandwagon under whose banner all sales executives are supposed to march. We are supposed to be terrified about what might happen to our sales organizations and results if we don't jump all in on sales enablement, yet several years in, even the movement's leaders have trouble articulating its defining features, core values, and best practices. Forgive my reaction, but to me, it feels like an academic discussion among intellectuals and a giant time-suck. Beware of any loosely defined group referring to itself as a society.

In 2017, account-based marketing and account-based selling became all the rage. Today's "experts" who have parked themselves under this newer umbrella promise us that account-based everything is the future of the sales profession. The only thing more common than articles about account-based selling are seeing sales improvement gurus rebranding themselves as ABS "experts." I haven't yet devoted the time or energy to look too deeply into this latest, greatest, best-thing-since-sliced-bread phenomenon. What I have read sounds intelligent and also very traditional. The customer should be our focus. We should be most concerned about the customer's needs, desires, people, processes, structure. And we, as sellers, should focus on aligning ourselves, our process, and our approach to the account. Account-based selling. Not exactly earth shattering. That's why several of my sales improvement friends are collectively scratching their heads, curious why so many gurus have chosen to go all in, hitching themselves to this bandwagon. ABS is so hot right now that every time I open LinkedIn I expect to find a listing of "The Top Fifty Must-Follow Account-Based Selling Influencers." By the time this book gets released, I am sure that top fifty list will exist.

More recently, there's been a rapid ascent of "experts" that Anthony Iannarino calls the Chicken Little Crowd. These fearmongers prey on the vulnerability of today's struggling and insecure sales leaders and sellers by proclaiming that the sales profession is going the way of the dinosaur and that the vast majority of the sales population will become extinct over the next decade and be quickly replaced by artificial intelligence. We have become unnecessary, superfluous vestiges of yesteryear. They say today's buyers don't require professional counsel. They cite "studies" that tell us these buyers purportedly go exactly 57 percent through their buying process prior to engaging with a salesperson, and that percentage will dramatically increase as AI bots grow in sophistication and popularity. Translation: All of us in sales are screwed, and we might as well throw in the towel now, freshen our résumés, and seek another way to earn a living.

Yes, I admit that I'm overstating their point. Yes, I know that McDonald's and other fast food restaurants are installing self-ordering kiosks to reduce the need for counter sales help. Yes, even many business-to-business, low-value, highly transactional sales now easily and painlessly happen online without the involvement of a salesperson. I get it. We are in the twenty-first century, and we have progressed as a people. The UPS driver trudges up my front lawn several times a week with deliveries from Amazon. com. No one is going to argue that technological advances have streamlined, and will continue to streamline, a buyer's ability to make purchases. But the sky is not falling on the sales profession. Operative word: profession. The professional seller, the one who delivers value, who proactively works into accounts before they are shopping, who seeks to truly understand a customer's needs, who does effective discovery work, who's motivated to solve a customer's problems, who tells a compelling story, who's committed to delivering valuable outcomes—that salesperson is not going anywhere anytime soon. In fact, most of the companies I work with are looking to add to their sales teams, not shrink them. And if a candidate showed up with the skills and attributes I just described, they would get hired in a nanosecond—faster than Siri or Alexa could say "artificial intelligence."

Strong Words for the #socialselling Charlatans and Their False Promises

Of all the trends and movements I've mentioned, none has been better promoted or more vigorously defended by its self-described founders, movement leaders, and "experts" than #socialselling.

That hashtag is there quite intentionally, and while I use it in jest and a lighthearted manner, it is there because the social-selling leaders put it there. It was a form of self-identification, and in some sense, the brand mark or logo of the movement itself. In fact, one of the foremost faces and most prominent voices even appeared to use #socialselling as the name of her firm.

Give credit where credit is due. The marketing of the #socialselling movement was brilliant. And it worked. Social-selling buzz spread like wildfire. It was All. The. Rage. Everywhere you turned, people were excited about social selling, and for good reason. Social media is incredibly powerful and social selling was promoted by those who had mastered platform-building on social channels. It made perfect sense that it would garner a large following. Plus, who didn't want it to be true? If I could tweet, connect, and comment instead of prospecting, why wouldn't I press the easy button and do that instead?

The really weird part for me is that I love social. I not only believe in it, I've benefitted tremendously from my very intentional participation on social channels over this past decade. I am a fan and a heavy user. But, and this is a very big BUT, it is not the magic bullet for salespeople that the leaders of the social-selling band claim it is. Social selling comes nowhere close to fulfilling the promises made by those *attempting* to make a living peddling its goodness. Even more concerning, not only do many social-selling "experts" lack credibility and a track record of personal success, but to further their own agenda, they also preach dangerous myths about the ineffectiveness of traditional selling methodologies.

Here's my rub. If social selling is the perfect panacea, the fix-all for every seller's sales shortfall, and the key to becoming a perennial high performer, then why are so many salespeople who rely on social-selling strategies opportunity-starved and desperate for help to fill their pipeline? If you've adopted social selling, shouldn't your pipeline be overflowing with new opportunities from all your mentions and retweeting on Twitter, all the perfecting of your LinkedIn profile, and your abundance of comments in LinkedIn groups and on posts?

If social selling is as effective as those strenuously promoting it claim, then why is the self-declared "creator of social selling" changing employers so often and, recently online, asking followers to help him find yet another new job? If his expertise and what he teaches are so powerful, shouldn't he be his company's most valuable employee and have other companies banging down his door to hire him to transform their sales organizations?

And if outbound prospecting is, at worst, dead and, at best, terribly ineffective, then someone please explain why one of the (maybe *the*) largest social-selling training companies, in its own job description for selling its social-selling training, states that the candidate will be expected to deploy outbound prospecting techniques?

I have respect for that large social-selling training company. Unlike many in the space, they are intellectually honest. They believe in using all approaches, all methods available to create sales opportunities. They are transparent about the fact that social alone is probably not sufficient to fill their own funnel, and in doing so they are telling you that social is not sufficient to fill yours either. That type of honesty is rare in the sales improvement industry.

Last year, I made the mistake of challenging a social-selling and inbound-only "expert" from overseas. His LinkedIn articles were becoming progressively more obnoxious and untruthful. He not only poked fun at and tried to embarrass salespeople who use traditional approaches (and quickly insulted me when I chimed in), he set up straw man arguments that redefined prospecting as something it is not. This is one prototypical example from one "expert" to illustrate an approach that has been rampant the past several years. I could fill this entire book with dozens and dozens of similar examples. I have nothing special against this person; his mindset and writing represent a very common approach, and his level of hostility makes him fair game to expose his silliness.

This "international bestselling author," whose book has a total of four Amazon reviews in his own country, dropped a "truth bomb" (his words) in a LinkedIn article that he cautioned would upset quite a few! (his exclamation mark). In the "truth bomb," he went on to say that successful salespeople in the future will "*never* risk annoying" potential customers with "dumb outreach" like mass mailings, autodialers, and cold-calling.

Holy overstatement-and-obscene-analogy, Batman. Do you see what this guy is doing here? He is trying to equate any type of prospecting or proactive outreach with spamming and telemarketing. That's not just unfair, it is wrong and absurd. Let's be crystal clear: There is a huge difference between telemarketers being fed random calls by an autodialer and what professional salespeople do when strategically targeting accounts and proactively initiating contact with people at those strategically selected prospective customers. Night and day. Apples and oranges. Totally unfair comparison. I don't know one single company that has salespeople blindly cold-calling the phone book.

Let me also take issue with something else he proclaims. Successful salespeople of the future will *never* risk annoying potential buyers? Really? *Never* is a strong word, wouldn't you say? It's also inaccurate. I can't speak for the future because I live in the present, but I can point to a whole lot of today's top-producing salespeople who have perfected the art of interrupting buyers. What do these high-performing sales hunters have in common? An absolute commitment to earn an early-stage discovery conversation/meeting with their target prospect. And if earning that all-important meeting includes risking that they may potentially annoy the buyer, so be it. That's life. Frankly, that is part of being in sales unless you live in a utopian fantasy world where you're continually handed more appointments and highly qualified hot leads than you could possibly pursue.

Great sales hunters learn how to pursue prospects in such a manner that they minimize the risk of being perceived as annoying. However, the fact that risk exists does not stop them from proactively hunting for new business. If it did, I'd make the case they probably are not cut out for a true sales role, but that's a topic for a much later chapter.

Getting back to our "expert's" truth bomb, later in that same article he takes his inflated argument a step further by quoting trusted marketing expert and renowned author Seth Godin:

"Selling to people who actually want to hear from you is better than interrupting strangers who don't."

Duh! Who's going to argue with that? Of course, it is *always* better to have a "tribe," warm leads, and referrals to pursue. But it is disingenuous to quote a legend like Seth Godin in this context. And this is the giant hole in the social and inbound-only argument these "experts" never address: What is the salesperson who doesn't have warm leads and enough opportunities to work supposed to do? Yes, it would be truly wonderful to have a tribe of loyal followers chasing you for information and help. But if your job is to sell (which I am pretty sure is every salesperson's job), and there is no one raising a hand asking you to sell to them, then what? Tweet more? Blog more?

Great question. I'm glad you asked. Astoundingly, there is yet another tranche of social-selling "experts" happy to provide the answer, vehemently making the case that to be a credible sales-person you must put out your own content and IP (intellectual property). I have read multiple articles from these misguided folks who, with no shame, tell salespeople that they would be more productive and better off writing blog posts or creating YouTube videos than picking up the phone. Read that sentence one more time, please. I want it to sink in that there are people running around claiming to be sales experts who, with a straight face, proclaim that *all* salespeople should be creating content and that most sellers would be better off writing and posting content than they would be deploying more traditional sales approaches like picking up the phone and asking a prospect to commit twenty minutes to meet with you.

This one dumbfounds me. It is hard to know exactly where to start the rebuttal. How about with the reality that only a small percentage of salespeople write well enough to even consider writing for public consumption? My intention here is not to insult the average seller, just simply stating the fact that after reading a whole lot of salespeople's emails and proposals, it is not a stretch to declare that writing is probably not their strong suit.

When I challenge the "experts" encouraging salespeople to crank out content instead of prospecting, they often turn around and call me a hypocrite because I benefit from creating content and putting out IP. On the surface, I understand the accusation. In fact, next to speaking with people who can buy from me, it's my single highest-value activity and what generates many of the inbound inquiries I receive. But this is where the paths diverge.

I am not a salesperson working for a company; I'm a consultant and author who gets hired for my intellectual property. My business is creating content for others to consume. It is neither fair nor accurate nor helpful to hold out people in my business as examples of what salespeople should be doing regarding content creation. If anything, my success as a creator and distributor of content is a very poor and misleading use case. I plead with salespeople not to follow my lead. Don't do what I do. Follow the lead of those having the most success in similar roles. Watch what top producers in your company or your industry are doing to secure early-stage meetings with potential customers and mimic their approach—whether it's prospecting by phone, attending association events, walking trade show floors, requesting referrals, or some other method. But unless you can find sellers in similar roles having tremendous success from creating and publishing their own content, I would be highly skeptical you'd be well served following that route.

Let me offer one more egregious example of how people ("experts") with strong agendas can be absolutely blind to reality or unaware how absurd what they are preaching is. This is a great illustration of how, at times, someone can only see through his own lens and so is incapable of seeing clearly because his livelihood is completely dependent on the lens through which he is looking. Just last month, the chief sales officer of a firm that touts its founding partners as the world's foremost social-selling experts posted something so bizarre and, in my opinion, so self-damaging that I cannot for the life of me comprehend that is *the message* their "digital sales transformation" company wants to send to the marketplace.

In a LinkedIn post with a selfie posing in front of an issue of *Forbes* magazine with Kylie Jenner on the cover, this chief sales officer challenged sales leaders who might be on the fence about social selling. He references the *Forbes* article on Kylie Jenner, who was about to surpass $1 billion in net worth, attributing her success to her ability to influence her gigantic social network.

Using this bizarre example, he attempts to make the case that based on her outrageous success how could anyone still wonder whether #socialselling leads to real sales. The post concludes with a dig that Kylie did not cold call her way to $900 million.

Friends, I present to you the unvarnished thoughts of the chief sales officer representing a firm of #socialselling experts who promise to transform your sales effort.

I don't know where to start the deconstruction of this post. It's wrong. It's cheap. It's silly. It's overreaching. It's blatantly disingenuous. It's dangerous. It nicely demonstrates why we should be very wary of the "experts," and it's a perfect picture of the untethering from reality and truth to which I referred earlier.

Can someone please explain why and how the meteoric rise in net worth of a B-list celebrity who lives on social media is an appropriate example to convince sales leaders their people should go all-in on #socialselling, or that salespeople should abandon prospecting in favor of Instagram and Twitter? Kylie Jenner's wealth is the basis to claim that #socialselling leads to "real sales"? She is the role model for people who want to become top-producing business-to-business salespeople?

I would love to see this chief sales officer and his firm rationalize the relevance of this example he's holding out for the typical pharmaceutical sales rep. Or the sales team at my defense contractor client. Or the construction equipment dealership. Or the salespeople selling 3M abrasives for a regional distributor. Or even my trendy tech clients in the data analytics or eco solutions space.

Oh, and nice throwaway line throwing shade at cold-calling to conclude the post. Classy. This "expert" could not have been more shallow and transparent. I am just thankful he published that post while I was writing this book, because that was a gift. I wouldn't have had the audacity to accuse someone of preaching something that foolish if I had not seen it. There you have it from the self-declared leading company in digital sales transformation: If you want to become a top-producing salesperson, ladies and gentlemen, Kylie Jenner is your role model, and you'd better start upping your selfie game. Yeah, good luck with that. Lemme know how it turns out for you.

Occasionally, someone online will ask why I'm so negative or nasty about social selling. So, I remind readers that my wrath is not directed toward social selling as a methodology or component of your proactive sales attack. I implore salespeople to use every appropriate, effective, and ethical means available. I'll say it again: I love social. I'm a fan. I benefit from it, and so can many sales professionals. My righteous anger is targeted purely and squarely at the "experts" and their nonsense that misleads and hurts the sales community. Whether it's the overseas "expert" making inaccurate, overreaching blanket statements and quoting credible sources out of context, this chief sales officer twisting himself in knots hoping to convince you that Kylie Jenner's approach should drive your sales strategy, or anyone else preaching such silliness, this stupidity deserves a response.

CHAPTER 3

Just Because It's Published Doesn't Mean It's True

Yes, we should be very wary of today's sales experts, and doubly wary when they're citing statistics or claiming credibility merely because they've been named to a "top influencer/blogger/consultant/author" list.

Call me a skeptic, but I feel like Mark Twain must have felt when he highlighted this quote attributed to British Prime Minister Benjamin Disraeli, "There are three kinds of lies: lies, damn lies, and statistics." The past few years, popular sales articles have been chock-full of all kinds of statistics about sales, sellers, buyers, you name it. Honestly, it's been hard to keep up with the plethora of sales research being quoted by experts, and it's been even harder to believe the "studies" they cite.

• • •

99 Percent of All Statistics Only Tell
49 Percent of the Story

No one states this better than Ron DeLegee II in *Gents with No Cents* (Half Full Publishing Group, 2011): 99 percent of all statistics only tell 49 percent of the story! That says it all, and is exactly how I feel every time an expert with an agenda quotes a favorite study in the hopes of convincing you that you need his solution for your sales problem. It's overdone, simplistic, highly transparent and, frankly, pathetic.

One of my leadership mentors, a friend and brilliant St. Louis-based consultant named David Kuenzle, often cautioned us about the danger of relying on averages. He loved to joke that if one of your feet is on a block of ice and the other on burning coals, then, on average, you should be comfortable. Well, 100 percent of us, without hesitating, would declare that theory ridiculous. But what if a well-regarded research firm set out to "study" this issue and came back with a report emphatically declaring that 57 percent of those observed with one foot on ice and the other on hot coals were indeed comfortable? Would we buy into their research? Of course we wouldn't. We have brains and we have experience. Regardless of how supposedly credible the institution doing the research, how well intentioned its authors, or how well written its study, none of us would believe that we would be comfortable in that position, because nothing about it makes sense.

So, please explain why, when CEB (acquired by Gartner in 2017) comes out in *The Challenger Sale* declaring its research shows that buyers progress 57 percent through the buying process before talking with a seller/supplier, a good portion of the sales improvement industry not only accepts that as gospel, but then, unchallenged, begins manipulating that stat to promote their own training/solutions/agendas?

For the past seven years, that 57 percent number has been the most overused and misapplied statistic in the sales business. Group-think sets in and that number is tossed around, repeated, and accepted as truth just like we accept that the Earth is round.

Everywhere I turned, there were sales "experts" quoting the 57 percent study. They still do today.

From day one, I believed it to be incorrect and said so publicly and often. Oh, I don't doubt that the research was valid and that the authors were only reporting on what their study observed. They weren't the ones with an agenda. But because I have eyes and ears and clients across a variety of industries (and geographies, not just in Boston and Silicon Valley, where many of the sales elites and nouveau experts live), I knew instinctively that there had to be holes or biases in the report. Why? Because in the companies I work with, the only time that silly statistic proves true is when there are lazy, reactive salespeople sitting on their butts waiting for a customer to approach them. In other words, there may be many situations where buyers, *on average,* get 57 percent through the process before engaging with a salesperson, but that certainly isn't the case where salespeople are proactively and strategically pursuing target accounts before the buyer is shopping. My clients' sales teams are getting in to see prospective customers, in many cases, before they have even progressed 10 percent down the buying path and sometimes before the buyer has even started shopping. These proactive New-Sales-focused hunters are out looking to create new opportunities, not simply to respond to buyers who summon them after getting, *on average,* 57 percent to the decision point.

The odd part here is that it's not the people who published the study (CEB) who have been constantly misapplying the conclusion. It is other sales experts twisting the data to fit their own biased narratives. One of the most dangerous myths—dare I say, lies—perpetrated by the charlatans misusing this research, is that it is fruitless to prospect and pursue your target accounts because "they won't even talk to you until they're 57 percent through the process."

Please shake your head with me as you read this, pondering the absurdity of a manager or executive (with a need) sitting at his desk with a flow chart outlining his buying process showing this giant firewall at the 57 percent mark. Before that firewall, this buyer's documented, formal process prohibits him from seeing or talking with a salesperson who might be able to help. It's ludicrous. We all know that type of formalized buying process is as rare as a rainbow, and those companies that do have one certainly don't place restrictions on when managers, executives, or even procurement people may engage with value-delivering salespeople who might actually be in a position to offer perspective, ideas, options, and more.

The reason this overused and misapplied statistic makes me so angry, aside from the fact that it is not true, is that it hurts salespeople, particularly struggling salespeople who are desperately looking for answers. When the struggling, gullible (or lazy), ill-informed seller with a weak pipeline hears prominent, manipulative voices in the #socialselling or inbound camps quoting the 57 percent stat and ridiculing people for even thinking about picking up the phone to call a prospect, bad things happen.

Think about it. This salesperson is likely already predisposed against traditional prospecting and there's a decent chance, like many sellers, he suffers from call reluctance anyway. He knows there are not enough opportunities in his pipeline to make his number, and just as he gets energized and prepared to do something about it, he makes the mistake of reading a LinkedIn article proclaiming that prospecting is dead, the phone doesn't work anymore, and buyers won't engage you until they are 57 percent through their process anyway. So at this critical decision point, he begins to think, why bother? Instead of doing something productive like actually calling a potential customer, he goes back to trying to perfect his LinkedIn profile, commenting on posts, retweeting others' content, and complaining that his company isn't providing enough leads. That sad scenario is why I chose to enter the arena and fight back publicly against those whose myths and biases are hurting the very salespeople they claim they're trying to help.

You Quote Your Study and I'll Quote Mine

Intuition and personal observations forced me to question the veracity of the 57 percent gospel and those benefitting from its widespread acceptance. Instinctively and anecdotally, I knew it couldn't be right, but was nonetheless relieved when more recent studies emerged painting a very different picture. As you might imagine, I was thrilled when newer research emerged backing up what many of us in the trenches observe every day.

In 2015, OpenView Labs asked me to pen an article (see https://labs.openviewpartners.com/67-percent-buying-process -before-sales-myth/#.XJJibS2ZOuM) in response to the release by SiriusDecisions of its own exhaustive research debunking the 57 percent myth and revealing that buyers are, in fact, engaging with sellers from the very beginning through the end of their buying journey (through the three stages SiriusDecisions calls "education," "solution," and "selection"). Their study looked at the buying behaviors of 1,000 B2B executives who were involved in significant purchase decisions during the previous six months (see a summary of the study at https://bit.ly/2DmPAp8).

SiriusDecisions's data and conclusions aligned exactly with

what I was witnessing across my client sales teams: Buyers interacted with sales representatives during *every* stage of the decision-making process, and in more than half the cases, salespeople were involved at the very beginning of the buyer's journey. In my article for OpenView Labs, I begged readers to take this study seriously and declared it was great news for those willing to take responsibility for creating their own leads instead of waiting for them to materialize.

Even more exciting news came from RAIN Group's Center for Sales Research in early 2018. To say that I smiled reading this report from Mike Schultz, copresident of RAIN Group, would be an understatement: "Previous outside research suggested that 57 percent of the purchase decision is complete before a customer calls a supplier and 67 percent of the buying journey is done digitally, giving sellers the false impression that buyers don't want or need to talk to them early in the buying process. Our new research reveals that buyers want to talk to sellers much earlier in the sales process and debunks many common myths" (see https://bit.ly/2FAmTY0). Preach, Mike Schultz. Preach.

RAIN Group's research across twenty-five industries also demonstrated that 82 percent of buyers accepted meetings with sellers who proactively pursued them, and that more than half the meetings secured were initiated by salespeople using the phone and email. For those of you who've been persuaded that traditional selling is dead, I encourage you to reread that last sentence. I know that data like this doesn't get a lot of play on the internet because *traditional* is not new or sexy, but if you've been poisoned by nouveau nonsense the past several years, this alternative perspective may be exactly what you need to hear.

While I was more than willing to rail against the misapplication of the 57 percent statistic based purely on common sense and personal observations, it was a relief when studies began emerging in support of what many of us already knew to be the case. The bottom line is that you should be highly skeptical of today's "experts," doubly skeptical of data they quote, and possibly even more cynical when they cite being named to some "Top Sales (Influencer/Consultant/Book)" list as a reason to trust them.

All Seals of Approval Are Not Created Equal

All of us in the sales improvement business love attention, and we particularly love being named to one or more of the dozens of "Top (fill in the blank)" lists published every year. I admit, right here and right now, that I have enjoyed and benefitted from the notoriety of being named to these lists. It's a nice ego boost and also fun to claim inclusion on these lists in your bio. Some of the list (wannabe king) makers even provide a little graphic or widget to post on your website showing off your status and, of course, promoting the organization bestowing you with such an honor.

It all seems harmless until you pause and pull back the covers to see which consultants and books are being named to these annual lists. Recently, a well-known sales publication released a list of top sales consultants. I was pleased to see several colleagues I truly respect named to the list but was beyond dumbfounded by others who were bestowed the honor. As I scanned this top sales consultant list, I had the same realization as when I peruse many of the top sales-books lists. These consultants and authors were either friends of, or supporters of, the list maker. One person named a top sales consultant had, only months earlier, just returned to consulting after bouncing from job to job many, many times over the past few years. These were not the top books or top consultants being named to these lists. Not even close. These were simply the people who promoted the platform and businesses of those supposedly credible sources publishing these lists. It's pathetic.

My message is simple: Beware. Beware of the experts, their data, their sounds-too-good-to-be-true quick fixes, and the sources and lists they cite as reason to believe they're credible. And as we shockingly learned in 2016, we should even be wary of the political experts and polling research, which (incorrectly) guaranteed with absolute certainly the outcome of the presidential election.

CHAPTER 4

Seven Powerful Sales Lessons from the 2016 US Presidential Election

AUTHOR'S NOTE: I am well aware that the United States populace has likely never been more divided than now, and that the controversial presidency of Donald Trump makes it challenging to look back objectively at the 2016 election. As someone who travels internationally, I have also experienced the perplexed and often fearful reaction to Donald Trump's personality, politics, and policies from citizens of many countries around the world, particularly in Asia and Europe. As you'll read in this chapter, I wrote-in myself for president on my 2016 election ballot, because I could not vote for either major party candidate. I have no political motive as I share these sales lessons from the election. I make no claim that what follows is a comprehensive explanation of the results, and I fully realize there were many other factors contributing to the outcome. My sole intention is to point out, from a sales coaching perspective, the important lessons sellers can take away from this bizarre election, because there is much we can learn and apply.

No, I am not crazy, and I'm not even going to violate my own iron law to never combine politics and business. I completely get the risk of even being perceived as "going political."

Please believe me: I. Am. Not. Going. Political. Remember, I'm the coach constantly reminding salespeople to stop posting their political views on Facebook or talking politics with clients and prospects because nothing positive will result from it.

I have no political agenda. And as you'll see shortly, I didn't have and still don't have a horse in the political race. But there are just too many powerful sales lessons to be gleaned from the stunning election of Donald J. Trump as president of the United States of America to not tackle this topic in a book looking at #SalesTruth. Besides, it is another amazing example of how badly wrong *all* the experts could be—even about something so big to which everyone was paying attention.

Let's get this out of the way right up front, because I can imagine the immediate, visceral, blood-pressure-raising reaction of 97 percent of Americans (and even many in other countries) from just reading the title of this chapter. I did not vote for him. And neither did I vote for her. In disgust and protest, I voted for someone of higher character whose real-world experience (and maybe his fantasy about having Air Force One as his personal transportation) and true love for his country, I felt made him a better candidate. I voted for myself.

The question, "Could we not do better than this?" was a regular dinner conversation topic with friends and family during the fall of 2016. One of my sharpest and most pithy friends, Brian Fogt (who also happens to be the top-rated golf instructor in Missouri and the teaching pro at Bellerive Country Club, where the 100th PGA Championship was held in 2018), may have coined the best phrase to sum up how most people in my circle felt. At a restaurant one evening as we bemoaned our choices, Brian deadpanned, "You know the expression 'the lesser of two evils'? Well, this election is really the evil of two lessers!" Perfectly stated, Brian. Two *lessers*.

Before unpacking the powerful lessons from the election, let me address four particular groups of Americans, all of whom are probably ready to throw stones at me for their own reasons:

> To the Make America Great Again Trump-lovers hailing his achievements while overlooking his gracelessness and trouble with the truth,
>
> To the #NeverTrumpers, who have lived every day since the election angry, bewildered, and hysterically fearful (and whose Twitter streams prove it),
>
> To the Hillary-lovers, who not only believe she's the smartest woman to ever walk this planet but that she also *deserved* the presidency,
>
> And to the venom-spewing Hillary-haters, who somehow found it acceptable to chant "lock her up" at political rallies, I say this:

> Stop it. For a few minutes, just stop it. Breathe deeply. Pretend, briefly, that we are all actually fellow citizens on the same team. Imagine, if possible, that the other side is not evil and that there might actually be intelligent, caring, good people who love this nation as much as you do on the other side of the political aisle.

Again, I am not making the case that these seven powerful takeaways represent a comprehensive list. I acknowledge there were many other factors that likely contributed to the outcome, and for all I know, Trump might not still be president by the time you are reading this. So, I'm pleading with you to compartmentalize your political passion and all the emotion surrounding the election and this presidency for just a few minutes, and open your mind to processing these very likely reasons that contributed to Hillary losing and Trump winning, because I see salespeople winning and losing deals and customers for these *very same reasons.*

So, how did it happen? How were the experts and polls so wrong? It is amazing that, similar to how no one holds sales "experts" accountable for their nonsense and false information, we didn't hear about political pundits and expert pollsters being fired after the 2016 election. Because if you remember the polls leading up to Election Day, a grand total of *none* predicted that Trump would win. *None.* One more reason to be wary of "experts" and their supposedly valid research.

Disclaimer and Full Transparency: I am not a political expert, and my political passions, leanings, and trust in politicians and parties have waned significantly over the last two decades. I've come to despise both CNN and Fox News, because neither attempts to provide us straight news. They both have stopped even pretending that they're impartial. We haven't put a sign for a candidate in our front yard for a very long time, because the last candidate we supported ended up getting arrested while in office—I kid you not. I'm a native New Yorker who's lived in the heart of the Midwest for twenty-five years, a guy with a Jewish last name who is a devoted Christ-follower compelled by God's grace, forgiveness, and acceptance. I attend an apolitical, multicampus church with a high social-justice value. Our pastors regularly remind us that God doesn't ride on the back of donkeys or elephants. I am also a small-business owner who has been forced onto an individual family ACA-compliant (Obamacare) healthcare plan, and I support a family of five, including three children simultaneously enrolled full time in three universities. I work with companies in a wide variety of industries, including some who manufacture product in America, and as someone who evaluates sales effectiveness and who coaches salespeople for a living, it is safe to conclude that I have some expertise and also strong opinions about what works in sales and what doesn't. So, with that as the backdrop and in full transparency about where I come from, who I am, what I do and believe, where I worship, how I get my healthcare, and for whom I voted, here is one man's take on some very powerful lessons for salespeople and sales leaders from the 2016 US presidential election that shocked the world.

People (Buyers) Act in Their Own Self Interest, and Your Messaging Matters

This is Sales 101. And maybe 201 and 401 and graduate-level sales education as well. It's not about you. It's about the customer. People make purchase decisions for their reasons, not ours. Prospective buyers have issues in their lives (or businesses). These issues are what occupy their time and attention. Sometimes, in sales, we refer to these issues as their *pains*. When I'm helping a company or a salesperson sharpen their messaging, what I call the "sales story," we spend a lot of time listing the customer's issues that their solution/product/service address. What problems are your prospects looking to solve? What opportunities are they seeking to capture? Which of their fears are causing stress or keeping them up at night? Where do they feel trapped? What frustrations are driving them crazy? What outcome do they most want to achieve?

Our sales story is our most critical weapon, and we will address its importance and how to make yours as strong and compelling as possible in chapter 10.

I am regularly preaching to sales teams that there is almost nothing we can do to increase effectiveness as much as fixing our messaging. That's not a controversial statement, and there's pretty much universal agreement that if we are going to succeed in sales, we need a sharp, customer-issue-focused, compelling, and succinct story. Creating sharpened sales stories is one of my absolute favorite activities as a coach and consultant, so I pay a good deal of attention to "messaging," whether it's in emails, sales literature, voicemails, presentations, proposals, or even thirty-second television ads by politicians that end with that goofy legal declaration, "I'm Mike Weinberg, and I approved this message."

Since there is no argument that sales success is directly tied to the effectiveness of our story/messaging, what were the 2016 presidential candidates' main messages? Before reading on, just pause for a minute to reflect back and see if you can remember the big themes they presented to the public. Take a minute to do that now.

Welcome back. Let's start by looking for Hillary's core messaging. I intentionally say looking "for" instead of looking "at." Why? Because that was one of her biggest problems! What was her core message? What key compelling story points did her campaign continue to hit home?

If you are struggling to recall the main themes of her campaign, that tells us something, doesn't it? The fact that she was all over the place and continually shifting core message points was certainly a problem. None of Hillary's big story points gained traction. But I would make the strong case that an even bigger story problem was not her shifting themes—it was the focus of the messaging itself.

#ImWithHer. She's fighting for us. I work hard. I sweat the policy details. I'm uniquely qualified. Stronger Together. She's breaking down barriers. Help her shatter the glass ceiling. He's disgusting. "You could put half of Trump's supporters into what I call 'the basket of deplorables.'"

Let's ignore that final deadly element of Hillary's messaging for a moment. We'll come back to it because there's certainly a lesson for sellers about trashing not just your competition, but also those who support or like your competitor. Putting the unfortunate (but revealing) *deplorables* comment aside, as you review the themes of Hillary's macro messaging purely from a nonemotional, unbiased, story-evaluation perspective, what do you see? How does it make you feel? Maybe most important, let me ask this: Who is the focus of her message? And as all buyers ask themselves while tuned in to their favorite radio station (WIIFM), "What's in it for me?"

Exactly. Not only was the core message hard to repeat because it was constantly changing (eighty-five different slogans tested), but the pieces we could remember were just not that gripping, and they lacked power. Why so? Because the focus was wrong! #ImWithHer is catchy and brings to mind President Dwight Eisenhower's "I Like Ike" slogan, but it doesn't mean anything. The other themes were nice, even attractive and, my goodness, Hillary may have been, in terms of experience, one of the most qualified presidential candidates in history. But because these messaging points were about the candidate, not the electorate (customer), they certainly were not going to capture the minds and hearts of those precious few open-minded, undecided voters.

Taking a look at the other side, Trump's message(s) were intriguing and unconventional, to say the least. Make no mistake, many components of his "story" were even more self-absorbed, more self-promotional, and more arrogant than Hillary's. Humility, self-deprecation, likability, and EQ (emotional quotient or emotional intelligence) are definitely not traits, themes, or tools in Trump's arsenal. I'm not sure I've observed a human being with lower emotional quotient than Donald J. Trump. My wife cringes at his every breath and move—whether speaking about his friends or his enemies, or awkwardly wiping dandruff off the suit jacket of another country's prime minister on live TV while telling reporters he is doing it. Honestly, I have to believe he makes even his most loyal, dyed-in-the-wool supporters cringe every now and then.

Let's look at the main story themes of Trump's campaign. What immediately comes to mind?

#MakeAmericaGreatAgain. I'm going to build a wall and Mexico is going to pay for it. Secure the borders. We will reduce the threat of terrorism by restricting access to the US from predominantly Muslim countries. Fix the trade imbalance by getting tough on our trading partners. Bring jobs back to the American manufacturing sector. Repeal and replace Obamacare. Drain the swamp. Reduce regulations on business. Lower taxes on corporations and the rich. We are going to win again; we are going to win so much you will be tired of winning. My opponents are idiots and all worthy of a label (Little Marco, Sleepy Jeb, Lying Ted, Crooked Hillary).

Everyone, take a deep breath and exhale. That's quite a list that likely creates very different reactions for different people. Nonetheless, those were the big themes and constant talking points of the Trump campaign. They were virtually the same from day one. He was extremely consistent and focused. A good sales story must be consistent and focused and his certainly was that and more. If you heard one Trump campaign rally, you heard them all.

Even more than consistent, however, I would argue that his "story" tapped into the hot-button issues that were top of mind for many, many Americans, Democrats and Republicans alike. While there certainly was much bragging about his own success and wealth, you cannot think back on Trump's campaign without "Make America Great Again" popping into your head (likely while picturing Trump wearing that rather unattractive red cap).

Whether you liked Trump or not, there is no arguing about the focus of that message. It was squarely on the customer. He was constantly beating the drum, reminding voters that he was going to tackle those big issues—many of which were their top concerns, fears, desires, and so on.

Speaking only for myself, I wanted better for America. I was ready to hear more about increasing our military strength and was concerned that President Obama had weakened the United States' position on the world stage. Like many who had grown fearful from seeing acts of terrorism committed on US soil, I certainly wanted to be better protected from terrorists potentially coming into the country. I did not appreciate Trump's tone or how he painted immigrants and refugees with such a broad brush, but I do believe the president's first priority is to protect our homeland. From a business perspective, as someone who works with companies that manufacture and sell heavy equipment domestically, the idea of leveling the trade playing field so my clients could compete more fairly with imported goods sounded attractive and was certainly relevant to me. I could also sense the restrained demand across many industries partially stemming from the Obama administration's heavy hand, increased regulation, and occasionally overt anti-business comments. And regarding a cause that is very personal to me as someone paying an obscene amount of money for my government-ordained "marketplace," very mediocre, "affordable" health plan, Trump's promise to repeal and replace Obamacare on day one got my attention fast.

A quick reminder: I didn't vote for the man. I am not endorsing his classless behavior or xenophobic rhetoric. I am simply trying to point out from a sales coaching perspective that the Trump message trumped Hillary's by a mile. We all knew and understood his "story." We could repeat it. For a lot of those swayable voters in the middle, the issues he touted were front and center on their radar. And as we all agree, buyers make decisions to further their own interests, not the seller's.

Think about your sales story and the message you are telling your customers and prospects. Is it all about you, or is it focused on the issues that matter dearly to them?

Don't Take Your Longtime, Loyal Customers for Granted

Just because they've been buying from you or your company for decades does not ensure that they will buy from you the next time. Circumstances change. People in key positions turn over. Sometimes the most loyal customers sense that their previously trusted supplier has lost its edge, or worse, has become complacent. I think it is pretty safe to say that all of these were true when it came to the Rust Belt states that had faithfully voted for the Democratic nominee up until 2016.

Writing the previous paragraph brought to mind that powerful United Airlines commercial from the very early days of my career. It was the 1990 one-minute spot referred to as the "Speech." The owner of a company gathered key associates and told them that he had received a phone call from one of their oldest customers who was firing them after a twenty-year relationship. "The customer said he didn't know us anymore, and I think I know why," the boss proclaimed. He shared his frustration that they were not having enough face-to-face contact with their customers as he lamented the fact that too much business communication was taking place via fax and phone call. The boss went on to tell his team, "We are going to set out for a little face-to-face chat with every customer we have," and as his assistant began handing out good old-fashioned United Airlines paper tickets to everyone in the room, United's theme song began to play. It's truly a classic ad, and I just got choked up watching it on YouTube as the inner sales guy in me was screaming, "YES!"

It's not a stretch to say that the Democratic "Blue Wall" in the Upper Midwest came crumbling down not just because Trump was preaching about bringing manufacturing jobs back to America. That wall of trusty "blue" states collapsed because Hillary virtually, and in some cases, literally, ignored those states, which ended up going to Trump.

The *Wisconsin State Journal* reported that Hillary was the first major party nominee for president to completely avoid the state of Wisconsin since 1972. Think about that. She didn't have the common courtesy to show up one time to say thank you, I care about you and your needs, and I need your vote. Not. One. Time. Wisconsin was so reliably blue—at least it had been since Ronald Reagan took its ten electoral votes way back in 1984—that she didn't feel compelled to campaign there. Trump ended up winning Wisconsin by seven-tenths of 1 percent. Seven-tenths. And the rest is history.

I'm usually the first to caution salespeople not to overserve existing customers, and that they'd produce more sales if they spent more time pursuing potential customers. Rocket science, I know. More time going after new business creates more new business. But Hillary took that concept to an extreme. There's a really big chasm between overserving and completely ignoring! She paid a dear price for taking traditionally loyal Democratic voters for granted. I guarantee that no presidential candidate will make that mistake again, and as sellers, we should take heed. It doesn't matter how long they've bought from you or how loyal your best customers have been. Things change. Your best contacts move on or retire. Internal power shifts. Competitors enter the market. Ignore your long-term customers at your own peril. Hillary did, and it may have cost her the race.

Prospects and Customers Do Not Always Tell the Truth

There were no polls predicting that Trump would win the presidency. Zero. It was hard to even find a pundit who dared to make the bold call for Trump. None of the polls pointed to this outcome. Following Election Day, there were more articles than you could possibly digest about why the polls were wrong and many plausible theories offered by pundits.

The theory I've come to believe is most accurate is that people simply didn't tell the truth to pollsters. Aside from my gut feeling, the best anecdotal evidence I have for this is my own lovely street in the section of the St. Louis suburbs known as West County.

I mentioned earlier that my family doesn't put political yard signs out during election season. What I didn't mention is that we may be the *only* ones on the street without yard signs. We live in a neighborhood that leans heavily to the right. *Heavily* might be an understatement. *Overwhelmingly* is probably the more accurate term to describe how politically conservative our neighbors vote. During any election season, of the dozens and dozens of yard signs on our street, 90 percent are for Republican candidates or causes. Having shared that with you, would you care to guess how many Trump signs dotted the lawns up and down our street of thirty homes? Exactly zero. Not one person admitted publicly they were voting for him. Not a single one. But the vast majority cast their ballots for Trump; they told me so—quietly. This little sample in Midwest suburban America was enough to convince me that people refused to tell pollsters the truth in 2016. Oh, just in case you are wondering—no, there were no signs for Hillary either. My friend Brian was spot on: the evil of two lessers.

The big sales lesson for us is that we should not automatically assume that what we hear from prospects and customers is true. It could be. Or, it could be partial truth. Or it could be completely false. It's not that most buyers lie to us intentionally. Sometimes, they are too nice (wimpy) and don't want to hurt our feelings if they are going to buy from someone else or if they have negative feelings toward our solution. Or, for their own reasons or advantage, they prefer to play their cards close to the vest. Or, like my neighbors, they have already made up their mind but don't feel obligated to disclose that to you. Or, possibly, they're not proud of their decision so they won't share it with you.

Whatever the motivation for buyers' lack of truthfulness or transparency with us, we need to do a better job discovering what is truly going on in our customers' world—more specifically, how, when, and why they make decisions. We must learn to be leery of surface answers. We should strive to build relationships with a wider array of people within the customer organization, so we don't end up pigeonholed by and beholden to one contact. We must better understand their internal buying culture and the landscape of competitors we are up against. And in the name of all that's good and holy in sales, we must, must, must conduct more effective sales calls that do a better job fleshing out potential obstacles and objections that could trip us up later in the sales process. The best time to uncover the customer's objections is always *right now*. In fact, the most confident and professional salespeople proactively bring up things that they sense might get in the customer's way of getting a deal done.

The Deal Is Won Before and After the Big Presentation, Not in the Boardroom or Convention Center

Call me weird, but I actually look forward to watching the huge political conventions when the delegates gather with pomp and circumstance to officially nominate the candidate who will represent their party in the general election. Maybe it's the funny hats and catchy banners or just seeing all the American flags. I enjoy the enthusiasm, the pride, passion, and the theatrical nature of the event.

There is one thing you can take to the bank every four years: The Democratic Convention will significantly exceed the Republican Convention in terms of production quality. It's not even close. Not sure if it's because the Dems have so much support from the Hollywood elites, or they're just that much better at putting on a show, but whatever the reason, their convention always blows away the Republican one. Never has that been truer than in 2016.

The Republican Convention was the week before the Democratic Convention in July 2016, and there is no way to say this nicely: It. Was. Bad. Hard to watch, and, at times, painful. It's not that it was choppy, poorly produced, and lacking luster—which it was. It just didn't work. Trump's divisive nature, lack of discipline, and tendency not to sweat the details all played into what we saw on television. The opening night's celebrity guest speakers were Scott Baio of *Happy Days* fame, soap opera actor Antonio Sabato Jr., and Willie Robertson of *Duck Dynasty*. Not impressed? Wondering if this is the best Trump could get? Same here.

It lacked the typical unity and coming together of the delegates. Rather than coalescing around the nominee, it felt like the battle had not been settled. Senator Ted Cruz, one of Trump's strongest contenders, did not even endorse him during his controversial speech on the third night of the convention. More than that, he went rogue, snubbing Trump by telling voters to vote their consciences. Not exactly the call to action you expect to hear heading into the general election battle. The convention was a failure. It bombed. There was no bounce in the polls for Trump coming out of it, and if it had been a big "finals presentation" in a prospect's boardroom attempting to win a giant deal, anyone would have graded it an F, and there would be serious thought to fire the salesperson and the sales manager who conducted it.

On the other hand, the Democratic Convention the following week was flawless and as highly produced and glitzy as you could imagine. Every *i* was dotted and every *t* crossed. It was perfection. The speakers beat up on Trump, not each other and their own candidate. Hillary's rival for the nomination, Senator Bernie Sanders, strongly endorsed her and encouraged his avid supporters to do the same. The final night was as well orchestrated and emotion-provoking as a blockbuster Broadway play. The only grade any fair observer could give this convention was an A. It was a home run.

Yet, Hillary lost in November, just three months post this phenomenal presentation.

Of the many sales lessons we can glean from this bizarre election, this is my favorite: *Presenting* is not a synonym for *selling.* In many cases, the presentation is only a small piece of the overall sales process, and its importance is typically overrated.

Contrary to what many slick-talking, silver-tongued-devil, uberconfident and superpolished salespeople believe, most big deals are not won in the boardroom by delivering pretty presentations. They are won by professional sellers who work their ass off prior to the presentation and frequently after presentation day too.

Particularly in larger, more complex, and longer sales-cycle deals, the advantage goes to the salesperson who does the best discovery work, meets with the most stakeholders and influencers, who best understands the various constituencies' needs and desires, and who builds both the best relationships and most consensus—all *before* presenting. It's worth rereading that last sentence several times, almost as if it's a deal-strategy checklist. Most salespeople skip all that hard work. They are either too lazy or possibly don't know how. Instead, they rely on gut instincts and their belief that they'll dazzle the customer with their polished presentation skills.

As the 2016 political conventions demonstrated, winning big on the big stage does not necessarily translate into winning the deal.

Don't Make False Promises or Name Your Product Something It Is Not

I am going to ask for patience as I make the case to pay attention to this particular lesson. This one is personal. You may have already sensed that I would head down this path based on what you're read so far.

Customers pay attention to the promises that sellers make, and they also tend to believe that a product's name accurately represents the product being sold to them. That's not unreasonable, is it? Well, as someone who is a "Marketplace" consumer of the Democrats' Affordable Care Act (Obamacare), I can share without reservation that the name of this product (program) in no way reflects reality. I'll share my own numbers to let you make the call if it is *affordable,* but it's not just individual purchasers like myself who have been victimized by the bait and switch. I have many friends and client business owners who have seen their health insurance premiums soar the past four years since Obamacare went into effect. They have been experiencing 25 percent premium increases every single year. When you do the math, their cost to provide health insurance benefits to employees has doubled. *Affordable,* eh?

I experienced the joy of applying for an individual family plan on a government-designed website. I will spare you the gory details of that awesome experience because you already know what a pleasure that must have been. What I won't spare you is having to look at my out-of-pocket cost for the privilege of participating in a very middle-of-the-road (Silver) Marketplace Plan. The annual premium for my family of five, comprising two fifty-year-olds and three children ages eighteen to twenty-two (health and pre-existing conditions are irrelevant and they don't even ask about that) is right at $29,000. That *affordable* Silver plan comes with a sky-high deductible and a $14,000 out-of-pocket maximum. Let me translate: I personally write $29,000 of checks to an insurance carrier for health insurance coverage and don't receive a penny of benefit until I have paid another $14,000 to cover deductibles. In effect, for the privilege of enrolling in a government-sponsored and mandated program, I get to pay $43,000 for my family's healthcare. I present to you the Affordable Care Act.

I don't need you to get out violins or shed a tear for me. Far from it. But I do hope that you get a sense of the rage that many of us who are actually funding Obamacare with our hard-earned money feel.

I also ask that you not leap to conclusions about my personal values or how I might feel about citizens' right to healthcare or the government's role in regulating it, and so on. I have a soft heart on this topic and think that in a country as big and wealthy and advanced as ours, no one, regardless of means or ability to pay, should be denied access to care. But I am also a realist, shaking my head and completely confused how anyone could think that this is either fair or *affordable.* Similar to other individuals and small-business owners who actually see and understand what they are paying for this health coverage, I am outraged. So, when it came time for the 2016 election and one candidate was talking about expanding Obamacare and the other was promising to repeal and replace it, I have a pretty strong sense of why people in the same boat I am would have voted for Trump.

What's the sales lesson? *Don't promise stuff you cannot deliver to your customers.* People have long memories. We were told very clearly, very loudly, and very often by President Obama and the Democrats in Congress when they were touting this healthcare legislation that we would be able to keep our plan, keep our doctors, and that premiums would come under control, possibly even decrease. The exact opposite happened.

In the wake of the 2018 midterm elections, it is interesting to see how many Republican weasels in Congress ended up facing the music for promising, alongside Trump, that their very first order of business on Day One of the Trump presidency would be to repeal and replace Obamacare. I clearly remember that promise on which they failed miserably.

Tell your customers the truth. Transparency is the best business policy. Don't make false promises when trying to win a deal, and don't name your product/solution something it clearly is not.

Trashing Your Competitor's Supporters Will Come Back to Haunt You

It's one thing to throw stones at your competition. I don't recommend it and typically try to avoid doing so, even when baited by the customer. But it is an entirely different thing to disrespect those who support your competitor.

I am sure Hillary and her speech writers were pretty jazzed

after coming up with the line that half of Trump's supporters belong in a basket of deplorables. I bet she was excited to use it to rile up her base and her supporters. After seeing crazed Trump supporters beating up protesters at his rallies and practically foaming at the mouth while chanting "lock her up," I am sure she was counting on being praised for pointing out the animalistic behavior of these lowlifes. All of that is understandable, but somehow none of these political geniuses thought through the potential unintended consequences from the woman who wanted to be America's leader publicly trashing a quarter of the population.

When you attack your competitor, people may excuse that because it is expected, particularly in politics. That's just the way the game is played. People, however, are not so quick to look the other way or forgive when you ridicule them personally. Once that came out of Hillary's mouth, there was no taking it back. For the rest of the campaign, she was on the defensive, working to restate what she meant by that statement and attempting to minimize the damage. But those words were very revealing about how she truly felt and also played right into the other side's narrative that she was not only disconnected from the perceptions, pains, and paranoia of many Americans, but had great disdain for them as well.

To make the business application of this lesson, imagine that you are working to dislodge an incumbent provider at a major prospect. Your prospective customer has been using your competitor's product/system/solution for several years. Within that company, there are both supporters and detractors of their existing provider. You do your very best to meet all these stakeholders and influencers to understand their current situation, their perspectives, their desired outcomes, and their feelings toward both your competitor's solution and yours. During your discovery process, you learn that there are a decent number of radical supporters of the existing provider, and they are really not interested in hearing your pitch or changing horses. This group is also rather vocal in expressing what you perceive as their unreasonable and irrational desire to stick with the status quo, despite its inadequacies and limitations.

For many reading this, I'm simply describing everyday life in your world. You regularly are forced to sell into hostile environments to people who potentially feel threatened by your presence and your proposed solution. What you definitely don't want to do is throw fuel on the fire and give these detractors more motivation to sabotage your sales effort. Can you picture the reaction if, during a big meeting with the decision-making committee, which includes members who support making a change and members vehemently opposed, the salesperson takes pot shots at the latter? In an effort to sway the group, the seller tells stories of other foolish, frightened, reactionary, backward-thinking customers who refused to upgrade their systems and now were paying the price. He ridicules the shortsightedness of those opposed to progress and makes fun of their fear of implementing a better mousetrap.

In doing so, the salesperson not only further alienates those on the committee who were against his proposed solution, he has created a mobilized force of mortal enemies who will stop at nothing to kill his sale. Instead of this being a business decision, it has become personal to those he has offended. This terrible sales move, while justified in the eyes of the seller, is exactly what Hillary did by proclaiming that a quarter of the electorate were "deplorables." That was a bad and ill-advised move for anyone looking to win friends and influence people. Thank you, Dale Carnegie.

To be fair, Trump did more than his fair share of insulting others. He was anything but classy and above the fray. He used inappropriate words, acting, at times, like a childhood playground bully. He dissed Senator John McCain, a Vietnam War hero and prisoner of war, saying, "He was not a war hero, because he was captured. I like people who weren't captured." He went beyond the pale in the disrespect he showed to a Gold Star (lost a child fighting for the US military) family who spoke at the Democratic Convention. He was downright mean to his Republican primary opponents and to Hillary. And we certainly cannot forget his constant belittling of the media, making them the scapegoat of almost every problem while declaring anything written or said against him as *fake news.*

The difference, I believe, is that while Trump continued to launch an all-out assault on his opponents, Hillary viewed Trump supporters as fair game. That is where the battle became personal to many voters, and it cost her more than she ever imagined when she uttered that deadly phrase. Salespeople, take heed.

Don't Count Your Chickens Before They Hatch (or Precelebrate Victory)

I was mentored very early in my career as a sales hunter not to spend the commission check before the deal was closed, the contract signed, and the invoice paid. That was sage advice from wily sales veterans who knew the pain and embarrassment caused by lighting the cigar and celebrating the giant victory prematurely. Nothing good comes when cocky sellers invest time and energy planning the victory party instead of working to the very last minute to close that deal.

Hillary experienced the pain of this firsthand. A week prior to the election, word got out about the enormous barge-launched fireworks display planned outside the Javits Convention Center over the Hudson River. The *New York Post* broke the story, starting the article with this intentional metaphor: "This could blow up in her face! Hillary Clinton may have lit the fuse for her victory celebration a little too soon." How prescient those writers were.

There was some blowback in the news about Hillary's plans, but in no way am I insinuating that the leak about Hillary's big celebration plans cost her the election or even any votes. I doubt it did.

It's highly unlikely that your customer would have any idea that you might be planning a victory parade, shopping for your dream car, or bragging about your pending huge win to peers or management inside your company. But I can tell you from first-hand experience, having seen salespeople do exactly that before losing a deal they were certain they'd win, that it is no fun and very costly to you personally when the deal you have been pre-celebrating doesn't come in.

Do not brag about your deal before it closes. Do not spend future commission dollars on something you otherwise can't afford, because you think the deal is a *sure thing*. Don't risk ending up with egg on your face. Instead, do the wise, mature thing. Work the deal to the very end. Never take for granted that it will happen or even go smoothly. Act like a professional who has been in the red zone before and knows exactly which plays to call to put the points up on the scoreboard.

I don't know whether you voted for *her*, for *him*, or, like myself, for neither. I don't know if you are ecstatic, horrified, or somewhere in-between about the election results and Trump's presidency so far. But I do know that these are powerful lessons that we, as professional sellers, can take away from Hillary's stunning loss and Trump's unlikely victory:

1. Remember that buyers act in their own interests and that your messaging (story) should not be about you but

rather about the issues you address for your customers and the outcomes you help them achieve.

2. Do not assume that your long-term, loyal customers will continue to buy from you. Be prepared to lose them if you take them for granted, or become complacent and leave the door open for competitors to gain a foothold.

3. Prospective customers do not always tell you the truth or fully reveal their intentions. Be leery of surface answers and do not be afraid to ask hard questions or bring up potential objections you may not be hearing.

4. Presenting is only a small part of the sales process, and big deals are often won by sellers who do the hard work of discovery, relationship building, and consensus building prior to, and after, the big presentation. It's foolish to count on winning based on your performance in the boardroom on presentation day.

5. Customers hear and will hold you to your promises. Don't make false claims and don't call your solution something that it clearly is not and never will be. There is a high likelihood that those deceptive practices will cost you dearly in the long run.

6. Speaking poorly about your competitors is unwise and speaking poorly about the people who like or support your competitor is stupid—and deadly.

7. You will never embarrass yourself working deals till they cross the finish line, but there is a good chance you will lose credibility and damage your reputation by prematurely celebrating deals that have yet to close.

PART II

The #Truth About Winning More New Sales

CHAPTER 5

To Win More New Sales Requires Focus on Winning New Sales

Scratching your head over the title of this chapter? I sure hope so. What I'm about to share with you is what I am compelled to tell executives, managers, and salespeople several times per week: The reason most salespeople (or sales teams) are not bringing in new business at the desired rate is because they spend very little time focused on bringing in new business. If that sentence has you wondering why you paid good money for a book with such commonsense advice, imagine how CEOs feel when I tell them the exact same thing right after depositing their check for my consulting fee.

It is not rocket science. It's freaking sales. You don't need an advanced degree, or really even much sales acumen, to come to the same conclusion. All you must do is watch how salespeople spend their time.

Don't Confuse Being Busy or Service Activity with Sales Activity

A typical, "very busy," industrial-type salesperson will spend a good part of the early morning socializing. For some, that socializing takes place at the office, maybe even right in the sales bullpen area. For others, they're being sociable online—checking Facebook, scanning their Instagram feeds, catching up with friends, or reading the news from their favorite online newspaper. From there, they transition to playing inbox jockey. Lots of emails to process. Ninety minutes (and a few cat videos) later, they're ready to get after it, but not until they deal with the customer service issues discovered in their inbox. Two good customers had questions about the status of open orders and another inquired about availability of a new product. After a quick run down the hall to see the customer service rep to check on his customers' orders, the sales rep pops over to the warehouse to grab a small order he offered to deliver that afternoon to yet another favorite customer. He shoots the breeze with the warehouse manager, and they talk trash about their upcoming matchup in the company fantasy football league.

Our "very busy" salesperson gets back to his desk in time to check email one more time before heading to the 10:30 a.m. sales team meeting. His sales manager intentionally scheduled this meeting every Friday from 10:30 a.m. to noon, so it does not interfere with the sales reps' high-value early morning activities (like prospecting and working to advance important sales opportunities in the pipeline), which, of course, our typical sales rep has expended exactly zero energy doing this particular (and almost every other) Friday. Following the sales meeting, a few of the reps head out for their typical Friday lunch at the local pub, and at 1:30 p.m. our "very busy" friend departs to deliver that small order to the customer. He arrives there at 2:30 p.m., spends a half-hour *relationship building*, and then leaves to pop in on another existing account that was looking for pricing on materials to be used in a potential project.

Many sellers, and even some managers, would consider that a pretty full sales day. There was direct interaction with several accounts and a few customer service fires were contained. One customer felt the love by getting a small order personally delivered by the salesperson, while another account appreciated the prompt response to a request for pricing. All of that accomplished in a day that also included a sales team meeting and lunch with the crew. What a feat!

Some may wonder, what's wrong with that day? I bet there are business owners and sales leaders who would be pleased with the sale rep's effort, responsiveness, service-minded attitude, and overall level of customer contact. Alternatively, I have a very different perspective. It is my strong belief that the primary job of a salesperson is to increase revenue, to create New Sales. So, while there is no argument that this seller touched a handful of customers, successfully resolved issues, and nicely serviced his accounts, I observed zero focus on proactively developing new business. What did this "salesperson" do that a significantly lower-paid customer service rep could not? Aside from possibly increasing customer satisfaction, what sales good was achieved? I'm serious. Where was the proactive sales activity? The focus on creating new sales? The intentionality to develop new business and grow revenue? It was glaringly absent here, and I often see the same elsewhere. Sadly, this is more typical than atypical.

Internal Meetings and Account Management Overload Do Not New Sales Make

It's not just the industrial-type seller who lives in reactive mode defaulting to an account, or territory management, mindset. I witness the same mentality and approach to time allocation in all types of businesses and sales roles. At a SaaS client, the senior account executives, who are the "hunters" for this company, each with a significant net new recurring revenue quota, spend (waste) an extraordinary amount of time in company meetings. It's a relatively small company, and it's understandable that senior management values these account executives' input. However, when you add up the cumulative hours these sellers spend in customer success meetings, product development meetings, all-hands meetings, new client onboarding meetings, the numbers are staggering.

As a whole, this team is falling short of achieving quota. From my seat, it's the opportunity cost from sitting in all those meetings that is one of the causes. I'm not suggesting that those meetings are unimportant or that the sales hunters' input isn't valuable. But we must consider the true cost of having our revenue creators tied up in non-revenue-creating meetings 20 percent of the work week.

Two years ago, I was called in to help reignite the sales effort at a very well-managed, successful, family-run business. I loved the people and their passion for the business. The company culture was healthy and strong. The sales team was talented and tenured. Their product and proprietary applications were top-notch, and their service to customers outstanding. The problem? After many years of solid growth, sales had plateaued.

What did I uncover? I found a truly dedicated, highly compensated, veteran sales team that for the most part was doing an outstanding job *managing* the major accounts that they had acquired over the past decade. And when I say *major*, I mean *major*—the biggest, baddest companies in an industry filled with household names we all know. These customers were very demanding, and my client provided them with a mission-critical application. There was a heavy account management burden on the sales team, and it was common that during any month, there would be a number of special requests or inquiries from customers, in addition to the standard administrative and account service tasks the salespeople handled.

I also discovered that the sales team members were not assigned goals for revenue growth. Further, there were no goals set for new customer acquisition. Sales results were not published. Sales management did not hold accountability meetings to review results with salespeople and obviously could not compare a salesperson's actual results against goals because there were no goals.

Additionally, billing customers at the end of the month was a lengthy, tedious, and manual process. The job of creating these custom invoices fell squarely on the salesperson. Due to the account executives' regular involvement with their customers and their intimate knowledge of custom projects that came in, my client's legacy billing process required members of the sales team to do all the prep work necessary to create invoices at month's end. For the salespeople with the largest accounts and most business, that process could take them up to two full days each month. Let that sink in. A company whose sales had plateaued had its very best sellers spending practically ten percent of the business days in a month working on the very glamorous, high-impact activity of preparing invoices. Oh. My. Goodness.

Wait. There's more. Have I mentioned that these talented, dedicated, experienced sellers were paid a generous commission on total revenue and that they were earning a significant income from *managing* the accounts already on the books?

It's not hard to see the case I am building here. No new business development goals. No sales reports. No accountability for bringing in net new business. A heavy account service responsibility. Two days per month spent on billing. Caring salespeople managing large books of business and large demanding customers. Fat commission checks coming every month rewarding glorified account management behavior and creating total complacency toward winning new sales. Even if these salespeople were proficient at hunting for new business, why would they? And when would they? When you're working your ass off managing existing relationships, not being held accountable or incented to acquire new business, why in the world would you take your eye off the ball servicing your current business to do the heavy lifting required to develop new business? You know the answer, and so do I.

Trust that I could fill the rest of this book describing and decrying the non-revenue-creating activities I see filling salespeople's days, weeks, and months. From the record-setting truck salesperson whose business began to slide because he was forced to sacrifice selling hours in order to deliver all the trucks he was selling, to the underperforming tech-company sales development rep who was more than happy to spend eight hours decorating for the company's Halloween party. It's criminal. And if it isn't a crime, it should be!

Salespeople are the forward-deployed troops, those soldiers on the very front lines—on mission to take new ground, to create new customer relationships, and to expand revenue within existing relationships. Assignments and tasks—no matter how important, whether voluntary or mandated—that take them away from their main mission hurt sales results in the long run.

To the salesperson who wants to start winning more new sales, it is imperative to spend the majority of your time executing the activities that actually create new sales. I'm not trying to be funny or condescending; I'm simply holding up a mirror for you. Answering customer service-type emails is not new sales-generating activity. Neither is running out a delivery to a customer. Nor is gathering the information necessary to invoice a customer. And volunteering to sit on committees or spend endless hours decorating for company parties is about the biggest waste of time I can imagine. Let your company find others who aren't responsible for driving top-line revenue to organize team-building events, chair committees, or trim the company Christmas tree. Everyone (including you and your family) is counting on you to do your primary job and do it well.

The people who preach that sales is service and service is sales are at worst dead wrong, and at best telling an incomplete story. I have seen no evidence that overserving an existing customer, particularly one that is not growable (more on that topic in chapter 9), drives new revenue. In actuality, the #SalesTruth is that I see the opposite. The salesperson who is trapped in an account management and service-first mentality is usually ranked at the very bottom when it comes to developing new business. My hope is that you will respond to this chapter by taking a long look at your mindset, your calendar, and your priorities. To get serious about increasing sales requires getting serious about where you spend your time and getting serious about prioritizing high-payoff sales behavior over customer service, account management, or good corporate citizen tasks.

To sales managers frustrated by their teams' poor performance relative to acquiring new relationships within accounts, acquiring new customers, new market share, or new business in general, I strongly suggest taking time out from your own typical, crazed routine to simply observe how your people spend (waste) their time. Your sales results shortfall might be as easily explained as your sellers having lost sight of their primary job—growing revenue.

Unfortunately, the sad reality is that often it's not the salesperson's desires or distractions keeping him from pursuing new business. In many cases, the problem is that the company views and uses salespeople as *free* labor to accomplish non-sales tasks, like the example of my client whose account executives do the month-end accounting to prepare invoices. It's not that their intention was bad, or that they were being cheap trying to avoid hiring clerical help. It's that their legacy processes blinded executives from the reality that having frontline, highly compensated members of the sales force working on invoicing is not the highest and best use of their time. Remember, this company brought me in because they had lost sales momentum. I didn't need an MBA or to be a McKinsey-trained consultant to point out their challenge resulting from having the sales team spending 10 percent of the month doing accounting and much of the other 90 percent *managing* accounts that were already giving them the lion's share of their business. That formula may be fine for maintaining what business you have, but it's an awful recipe for growing sales, particularly new sales.

CHAPTER 6

The Most Valuable Salespeople Don't Chase Opportunities, They Create Them

L ast September, I was in Germany facilitating a meeting with regional executives from Teradata. Typically, I don't publicly name my clients, but this situation is different because Teradata senior executives have been very public about the work I've been doing with the company. I share more about this engagement, Teradata's very talented sales executives, and their commitment to investing in frontline sales managers in chapter 16.

The purpose of this meeting in Munich was to customize the agenda for upcoming *Sales Management. Simplified.* workshops with their international sales leaders. As we were reviewing the common sales management sins that cause sales teams to under-perform, I displayed a slide picturing a salesperson waiting for a phone call while staring at her watch. As I described the damage done by managers allowing salespeople to live in reactive mode while waiting for an opportunity to find them, Andrew Blamey, the Australian executive over much of Asia-Pacific, said it better than I ever have. "Damn it, mate! We call our sales force the De-mand Creation Team. Their job is to create sales opportunities, not just respond to them. If we wanted them sitting on their ass waiting for opportunities, then we would call them the Demand Fulfillment Team."

Friends, that is sales leadership brilliance made even more memorable with an accent from Down Under. Andrew perfectly and succinctly stated one of the most damaging issues in sales today. Way too many salespeople believe that their mission is to chase and then close opportunities, and the result of this incorrect mindset is devastating to sales results.

Waiting for Opportunities Puts You at a Competitive Disadvantage and in a Weak Position

For years, I have been ranting about the dangers of salespeople being "late to the party." I've addressed it in multiple blog posts, guest articles for other publications, in my books, and in every workshop or training session I have led. This particular issue is that important, that widespread, and its consequences are that damaging.

Here's the deal: When sellers live in reactive mode waiting for opportunities, it guarantees that from the moment they are involved they are playing catch-up to a game already in progress. In many cases, they are forced not just to catch up to the buyer who has started down the path on the buying journey, but possibly also to competitors who either found the opportunity first or, even more deadly, created the opportunity with the customer through their own proactive sales efforts. It is bad enough being forced to play the game by the customer's rules but another thing entirely to be stuck playing by your competitor's.

That situation is no fun. Instead of defining or shaping the buyer's process and criteria, the seller is now trapped into merely reacting. Worse, the competitor who got there earlier has the advantage and is likely already strategically leading the customer down a path, even laying traps and creating obstacles to protect the competitor's position. If it is the type of big purchase that may result in an RFP (request for proposal) being issued, the competitor puts fingerprints all over that thing and works to stack the deck in their favor, basically assuring that their proposed solution will score highest. Ouch.

It is infinitely harder to influence the buyer's specs and decision process when you're late to the table. What is so odd to me is that just about everyone in sales agrees with that perspective. Salespeople never argue that point, and they admit, without reservation, that it stinks when you have to play your customer's or competitor's game. Yet, most sellers rarely change their behavior or fully commit to doing what is necessary to get out in front of sales opportunities. It's as if they are more comfortable doing "demand fulfillment," as Andrew Blamey termed it, even though they recognize the disadvantageous position it leaves them in.

Warm Leads and Set Appointments Should Be Viewed as the Icing, Not the Cake

True sales hunters and top producers take responsibility for filling their own pipeline with opportunities. They know that a full, healthy pipeline is the key to consistently bringing in new business, and these quota-crushers never make excuses or blame others when their pipelines are weak. They look directly in the mirror and say, "It's on me to put more into the top of the funnel." That response is very different from the typical underperformer with a weak pipeline who, instead, plays the victim card and puts more energy into pointing fingers and blaming others for his lack of opportunities than he does working to create them for himself.

Today, however, with the advent of sales development representative (SDR) and business development representative (BDR) roles, many salespeople have become dependent on being handed appointments. I get it. Who wouldn't want "free" appointments and warm, qualified leads served up on a silver platter? That sounds fantastic.

While real hunters love a freebie or a quality lead as much as the next guy, they never depend on someone else to fill their pipeline or portray themselves as victims. The perennial winners in sales roles work all stages of the sales process, from the top of the funnel to the bottom, and never take for granted that the top of the funnel has enough going into it. When they sense, for even a second, that their lead or appointment flow isn't what it needs to be to hit their sales goals, they immediately spring into action and laser-focus on creating new opportunities. For real sales hunters, this is an instinctive, almost reflex, reaction. The moment they sense an insufficient pipeline, they turn into new-business-development animals deploying all means to refill their sales funnels.

Last year, I led a two-day new-business-development workshop for a specialty consulting firm on the West Coast. What a treat to work with this company. Great culture. Proud heritage. A highly engaged executive team. True consultative sellers. Fun, outspoken people. We had a blast. The two days flew by.

During day one, we got into a "healthy discussion" (debate) about the role and effectiveness of the company's BDRs. There were widely varying opinions about the quality of the leads and appointments the BDR team was contributing to the sales team's funnel. As you might imagine, there were also differing views about how dependent the sales team members should be on appointments produced by the BDRs. Then, at just the right moment, as the weaker salespeople's complaints had devolved into whining, a top-producing, true-blue sales hunter, with perfect tone and a bit of attitude, dropped this gem on the room:

> **"Appointments set for us by the BDRs should be viewed the same way we view the Social Security portion of our retirement income—as gravy. We'd better not be counting to live off of it."**

There you have it. I've never heard it expressed better. I doubt that many who earn a living in sales are "hoping" or counting on Social Security payments to sustain them in retirement. Similarly, I don't know a single A-player sales hunter who lives completely dependent on others (or the company) to provide sales opportunities to keep the funnel full.

Yet, so many salespeople live passively every day in reactive mode, hoping, even expecting, a steady stream of good leads to be served up. This is 180 degrees opposite of how top-producing, consistent quota-crushers operate. Sales winners take personal responsibility for keeping their pipelines healthy and full, and do whatever is necessary—including prospecting—to make that happen.

The Keys to Becoming a Sales Opportunity Creator

I realize that many sellers and sales leaders resonate with the themes I am presenting and sincerely desire to make the leap from opportunity chaser to opportunity creator for themselves and their sales team. You read this and you want to become a demand creator, and in the process become more valuable to your customer, your own company, and the marketplace. Believe me when I say that there are no underemployed true sales hunters. People who have mastered creating and closing sales opportunities are in high demand and command top dollar. There are lots of people in sales who can fulfill demand but far fewer who can create it.

I've experienced the rewards (freedom, income, choices, etc.) from having been a top-producing hunter, and I so badly want you to experience the same. In my opinion, there is nothing more powerful you can do to increase your effectiveness and your earnings as a professional salesperson than to become highly proficient at the three critical phases of any sales process: creating, advancing, and closing opportunities.

We will touch on advancing and closing in later chapters, but first, we must dive deep into the keys to create new opportunities that fill the top of our sales funnel. Unfortunately, these keys seem to get the least attention from sales authors and trainers, yet they are absolutely foundational for becoming a consistent top-producing rainmaker:

- The Right Attitude
- Intentional Calendar Management
- Strategic Targeting
- Compelling Messaging
- Commitment to Prospecting

We will unpack each of these keys together over the next five chapters, but before moving ahead, take a few minutes to reflect on this list. What do you believe about prospecting and your ability to create opportunities from scratch? Do you truly have your prospects' and customers' best interests at heart, and is your motivation to sell pure? How well have you been using your calendar to plan your days and weeks? Have you been blocking time to work specifically on developing new business? Is opportunity creation a priority for you and, if so, where's the proof in your time allocation? Where is your finite, strategic list of target accounts that you are absolutely committed to proactively pursuing? How sure are you that those are the right accounts? How confident are you in your sales story? Is your messaging compelling, relevant, and effective at getting a prospective client's attention, building credibility, and opening the prospect up to dialogue with you? Do you have prospecting tools and techniques that work? Have you made the effort to become proficient at using the phone, yes, the good old-fashioned phone, to secure meetings with target prospects and customers?

I am asking you to acknowledge and commit to the reality that this is going to take work on your part. The #SalesTruth is that top-producing salespeople in every industry have mastered these five aspects of opportunity creation. If you want to up your game, or possibly experience breakthrough results for the first time, then you need to master these areas too.

I shared as emphatically as I know how in part I—There. Are. No. Shortcuts. To sales greatness. Spend time now reviewing these questions, take a personal inventory of where you stand today, and get yourself ready to get to work. We've got opportunities to create and New Sales to win.

CHAPTER 7

The Right Attitude Toward Developing New Business Changes Everything

I was in my midtwenties when I took my first sales job. My father, a big-time New York City sales executive, was amused because, all through college and in the first few years of my career, I made it very clear that I would never be a "salesperson." I chuckle now thinking back about how off-target my prediction was.

Dad sat me down before I left New York for St. Louis to become a territory sales manager, an assignment that included covering Walmart, my company's largest account. Back in the early 1990s, it wasn't popular to move to Northwest Arkansas to manage the Walmart business. People would instead choose to be based in a different city with easy access to Bentonville. Today, of course, many salespeople relocate to Rogers or Bentonville because it's not only a beautiful area, it's become quite the metropolis and a great place to live. I chose to relocate to St. Louis for several reasons, and twenty-seven years, the best wife on planet Earth, and three kids later, it is safe to say that decision worked out for me.

We Must Want the Best for Our Customer

Honestly, I don't remember most of my father's "sending me off to St. Louis and into sales" speech, but he gave it his best to impart as much wisdom into his twenty-five-year-old son as he could. There was one major point he shared that day that I will never ever forget. He made me look him right in the eye as he smiled, pointed at me, and said, "Your number one goal in sales is to make your customer as successful as possible. As long as your motivation is to help the customer win, you will always win in sales." Truer or wiser words have never been spoken.

When you have your potential or existing customer's best interests at heart, your motivation to sell is pure. Sure, you want the sale and you will benefit from making the sale. But as my dad so eloquently stated, when you are truly motivated to help your customer win, everything changes for you—particularly when it comes to the hardest part of selling, prospecting to begin the process of creating new opportunities.

Motivation for prospecting is all about perspective and how you see yourself, your solution, and your company. When you get your head and your heart right about *why* you should be working hard to create opportunities, prospecting becomes easier. Instead of dreading the fact that you are pursuing conversations with people who might avoid or resist you, you actually look forward to it, because deep inside, you know they need you and that you can help them.

This is what I consistently preach to help sellers form the proper attitude going into prospecting for new business:

You (and/or your company) are experts, problem-solvers, solution-providers, and value-creators for the customers/markets you serve.

Do you believe that? Do you truly believe that you (and others at your company) and your product/service provide great value? That you address a prospective client's issue or need? That the client's business, situation, or life will be improved by working with you/your company? That you really do solve a problem, reduce a liability, lower a cost, improve profit, speed production, remove hassles, increase (fill in the blank), or create a better outcome?

In the name of all that's good and right in business, I sure hope you can answer those questions in the affirmative. Because when you believe with conviction that the customer likely needs you/your solution and that you are, in fact, in a position to help, this very important benefit accrues to you as a seller: You actually want to prospect for new business and are driven to create new opportunities!

That's right. When you truly believe that you're the best option for the prospect and that you'd be remiss and irresponsible not to make every effort to secure a discovery meeting, your attitude about "interrupting" prospects changes. When you know the prospect is in danger (like a little kid about to run into the street), or is suffering with a suboptimal solution, or is stuck, confused, or unknowingly lost, it actually compels you to initiate contact—for the prospect's own good. You are not calling to bother; you are calling because you believe you very likely have the solution that will produce a better outcome. What could be a better and more pure motivation for wanting to meet with a prospective client?

Everything changes when you are driven to help your potential customer. Instead of prospecting feeling icky and like it's beneath you, it becomes a passion. Whatever reluctance or discomfort you may have initially had about stepping out to create your own opportunities goes away once you transform your attitude about prospecting.

Another huge benefit from adopting this mindset is that your prospects not only sense your passion to help them, but your authenticity. For lack of a better way of saying it, they can *smell* that you have their best interests at heart, not just your own. Nothing will set you apart from the jokers and manipulators in sales faster than you being perceived as someone who cares deeply about providing the absolute best possible outcome for the customer.

The very best salespeople I've observed initiate contact with a prospect convinced that the prospect needs them and would be foolish not to accept a meeting. And that, my sales friends, is exactly the mindset I desperately want you to adopt. When you do, it will position you to create more new sales opportunities than you ever believed possible.

We Must Believe That Proactively Initiating Contact with Prospective Customers Works

What we believe has a huge impact on how we perform. Just like in sports, what's going on between our ears affects what our body does. As I, and I'm sure many of you, can attest, it's pretty darn hard to drive a golf ball down the center of the fairway when your mind is screaming "duck hook" or "banana slice" during your backswing!

To succeed at self-generating your own sales opportunities, deep down, you must believe that it works. I know that prospecting works because I have done it myself for years. While working in various industries, I acquired new customers all over the United States through my personal prospecting efforts. I can point you to the specific buildings in Chicago, Chula Vista, Kansas City, Memphis, Miami, Temecula, and many other cities where

I scratched significant business out of the dirt. Without leads, without advertising, without brand recognition, without an inbound marketing campaign or social selling, I prospected my way into strategic target accounts, filled my pipeline with self-generated new opportunities, and closed record amounts of new business. Much of the success in my own sales career can be credited to a relentless commitment to filling the top of the sales funnel. This isn't my opinion or some theory. It is fact. It's #SalesTruth backed by significant evidence.

It is not just my own sales experience testifying to the fact that prospecting is an effective method for filling the pipeline. I have witnessed the same with dozens of sales teams and hundreds of salespeople. At a software-as-a-service (SaaS) company where I'm currently consulting, more than 80 percent of the new deals won were initiated from the proactive sales efforts of the account executives, not by the company's marketing engine. Let me repeat that, because I need you to have the same conviction that generating your own new opportunities absolutely works: In 2018, despite the nonsense and noise propagated by much of the sales improvement community and the faux "experts" telling us that prospecting is a complete waste of time, eight out of every ten new deals won by my client with a SaaS offering were generated by the sales team members' personal prospecting efforts.

Full STOP. It is not enough for me to believe that you can create your own new sales opportunities. YOU have to believe it.

The reason I'm being so dogmatic and repetitive in driving this home is because I know there is a good chance that this is messing with your worldview. It certainly conflicts with the popular sales teaching of the day. But for you to master creating new opportunities, you must believe with absolute certainty not only that you *can*, but that you *will* succeed doing it. That is why in chapter 2, I went so hard after the nouveau "experts" and their popular, but false, teaching. Sure, what they are preaching is attractive. I would love it if modeling Kylie Jenner as an example of how you should be social selling instead of prospecting was true. But you know it is not. I know it is not.

If you want to master winning more new sales, it requires mastering creating new opportunities. The first keys to doing so are getting your heart and your mind right. When your motivation is to deliver the best possible outcome and help the customer win, and you believe with certainty that your proactive efforts to contact prospects will be effective, good things follow.

CHAPTER 8

Take Back Your Calendar to Become More Selfishly Productive

The word *selfish* gets a bad rap. It makes sense why it does. Parents and teachers are constantly instructing children not to be selfish. From the moment we are old enough to listen and obey, we are taught to share. Share our toys. Share our cookies. Give someone else a turn. Play nice. Don't be selfish. Now, as adults, we are asked to share our calendar and to be good team players and responsible corporate citizens.

It all sounds great. I mean, who could possibly be against such a universally accepted teaching? That would be like coming out against the Golden Rule. Well, since you asked, I am against it. I am vehemently against the anti-selfish message when it comes to selling and salespeople, and I believe we'd all be better off if we stopped *sharing* our calendars and our selling time! I am also ready to torpedo the next human resource person who tells us that we need to hire a nice, collaborative team player for an open sales hunter role. I'll hold off on that one because sales talent and recruiting are an entirely different topic that we will address in chapter 16.

The #SalesTruth is that the highest performing salespeople are selfish. Top producers are selfish in a good way; they are *selfishly productive.*

To help unpack exactly what I mean by *selfishly productive* and why this is such an important concept relative to winning more new sales, I am borrowing from my closing message in the book *Sales Management. Simplified.* In the final paragraphs, I exhort managers that to create and maintain a healthy sales culture and continually drive increased results, they need to forcefully regain control of their calendars and remain laser focused on their highest-value activities. I've slightly edited the wording in the excerpt below to address salespeople as opposed to managers:

The most successful, productive, effective salespeople exhibit a characteristic that I've termed *selfishly productive.* They are incredibly selfish but in an incredibly good way. These highly effective sellers are ruthless with their time. They jealously guard their calendars and protect their time as if it's their oxygen supply. They become absolute masters at saying that simple two-letter word: no.

Selfishly productive people outperform others for one simple reason: They maximize their time on high-value, high-payoff activities. These highly effective sellers time-block their calendars, filling up their days with undertakings they feel are most important. Time blocking serves both a defensive and offensive purpose. From a defensive posture, filling your calendar with what you know you should be working on prevents that space from being available to others. It's freeing and energizing when someone invites you to a nonessential meeting to look in your calendar and see the time *already* reserved by you. "Sorry, I'm booked that afternoon with a high-priority activity."

As an offensive weapon, time blocking also ensures that you have sufficient time carved out to invest in those high-value activities you've identified. You feel empowered when you take back control of your calendar. There is this wonderful feeling that comes from deciding for yourself how you will spend your time.

Whether you're a senior executive, a sales manager, or an individual producer, the concept of being selfishly productive applies. For a salesperson, it may be most critical because there are so many others, both inside and outside your company, looking to give you *work* to do, much of which has nothing at all to do with creating, advancing, or closing sales opportunities.

Please invest some additional time considering this statement again:

Selfishly productive people outperform others for one simple reason: They maximize their time on high-value, high-payoff activities.

As crazy or simplistic as it sounds, that is what separates many top producers from the crowd. They know exactly which activities move the needle, and they selfishly guard and manage their calendars to ensure those activities are prioritized.

Highly effective, high-performance managers and salespeople spend the most time doing the precious few things that drive results, and they ignore, avoid, or delegate less essential tasks. Just typing that last sentence energizes me. I'm curious for your reaction. How much more energy would you have every day if you could radically increase time allocated to results-producing activities and strictly limit time wasted on tasks that did not progress you toward your big goals?

Time Blocking Is Transformational

I know of no other single technique with the potential to have such a transformative effect on productivity and performance. Even better, there is not an easier to grasp or easier to implement concept than time blocking.

Time blocking is neither new nor sophisticated. It is as old as the hills and a term that gets tossed around a lot but rarely adopted on a widespread scale. When I teach the concept at workshops, everyone agrees how powerful it would be, yet few adopt it wholeheartedly. Habits, legacy ways of operating, and lack of discipline rear their ugly heads and interfere with salespeople who buy into the concept intellectually but lack the commitment to implement it in practice.

My definition for this business- and life-transforming technique is quite simple:

Time blocking is the discipline of making appointments with yourself to work on your highest-value, highest-payoff activities.

No, it's not a quadratic equation or even long division. It's simple addition. We take back control of our calendar by getting to it first. We fill it with predetermined high-value activities that deserve and require more of our time, attention, and focus. We treat those scheduled time blocks as if they were as critical as a meeting with our own CEO or the most important person at our most important customer. In other words, we keep the appointment that we made with ourselves regardless of our feelings at the moment or what other urgent crap might be hitting the fan.

There is one extremely important presupposition in my definition: We must know what our highest-value activities are. You can time block every second, but if you are not getting activities that drive results into the calendar, then what's the point?

What are your three or four highest-payoff tasks? I cannot answer this for you; only you can for yourself and your role. Please grab a pen and pad and your favorite beverage—warm or cold, caffeinated or alcoholic, carbonated or *sin gas* (as my Latin American clients say), and spend some time listing out what you believe to be those precious few activities that will increase your performance. Don't shortchange this exercise. Take your time, because what you conclude here will be driving what goes into your calendar.

How did that go for you? For some sellers, it is a painstaking exercise as they have trouble identifying which three or four things truly drive the business. Others find this quite easy and rattle off their list in ten seconds flat. Whichever your situation, I encourage you to review your list with others—and particularly with your direct boss. When you work for yourself, you obviously don't need someone else's buy-in, but those who report to a manager or executive would be wise to seek input. Things tend to go a lot smoother when you and your leader agree where you should be spending your time, and just as important, where you shouldn't be spending it.

Unfortunately, there is not a cookie-cutter formula for creating a high-value activities list. Depending on each salesperson's current situation, existing account load, service requirements, sales goals, sales cycle length, sales process complexity, number of prospects, and other company-mandated tasks, every seller's list could be slightly different. Having said that, however, three big general categories should certainly serve as a guide: Sellers need to *close* hot opportunities, *advance* active opportunities, and *create* new opportunities. These three *Sales Verbs* should always be top of mind. Close. Advance. Create. No one would argue the fact that sellers who find ways to fill their calendar with more time dedicated to closing, advancing, and creating opportunities will outperform those who don't.

A Counterintuitive Approach to Create More New Opportunities and Maintain a Healthy Pipeline

Before you begin committing your high-value activities time blocks to your calendar, let me challenge you with a counterintuitive piece of advice. Time blocking is powerful and wonderful and transformative, and I'm 100 percent certain that your results will dramatically improve as you take back control of your calendar to spend more time working on the things you know move the needle. But the reality is that almost all salespeople default to working their hottest opportunities first. It makes complete sense why we would. Those deals are closest to the finish line and we can practically taste victory. So, instinctively we start our day with the activity, frankly, that's easiest and also *feels* most important. Unfortunately, in this case, our instincts are wrong.

Our first and best effort is typically spent working to *close* our hottest opportunities. From there, we progress up the funnel and begin working to *advance* existing active opportunities. Those are the deals that are in progress, where the customer has interest, and we expend energy to move these opportunities forward, or down the funnel, to where we can then shift to closing them.

There is a huge underlying problem with the approach just outlined, and it's not easily recognizable. Do you see it? When we approach this intuitively, it's very hard to spot. What could be wrong with first focusing on deals you're closest to closing and then shifting attention to work the next warmest opportunities? Well, when we do that, which segment of the funnel and which sales verb gets ignored? Exactly. The consequence of the hottest-first approach is that proactively working target accounts to *create* new opportunities gets shortchanged, or more likely, ignored. Most salespeople never get to it.

In contrast, people who consistently bring in new business are obsessed with pipeline health. They know that to maintain a constant flow of deals, their time and attention must be spread across all stages of the funnel and they cannot simply default to working opportunities at the bottom.

Top producers understand pipeline cause and effect. To them, it is logical that if you don't invest the appropriate effort to create new opportunities, then there won't be enough deal flow from the top down to the lower sections of the funnel. Said better,

Top producers prioritize the top of the sales funnel because they know that doing so ensures a healthy, balanced pipeline.

My strongest coaching to help you achieve breakthrough success in developing more new business is to prevent you from doing what most sellers do. Resist your instinct! Do *not* default to working your hottest deals first. Do. The. Opposite. Become the salesperson with the fattest, healthiest pipeline by intentionally prioritizing top of the funnel opportunity creation. How do you do that? It's as simple as can be. Put your prospecting and opportunity-creating activity time blocks in your calendar first. Even better, schedule them first thing in the morning.

There are several advantages to blocking early morning time for new business development. First and foremost, it actually gets done. Instead of putting it off until later in the day when it's much more likely to get trumped by something more urgent (or more attractive), get it out of the way first thing. Early morning outbound calling and messaging also allows you to reach prospects before they're distracted or overwhelmed by the crap hitting the fan in their world too. Another benefit from starting your day by attacking opportunity-creating activities is that it frees you up to focus, guilt free, on all your other responsibilities for the balance of the day. I would not be so harsh in criticizing salespeople for running deliveries to customers or scrambling to put out customer service fires if they had already invested a couple hours focusing on new business development earlier in the day.

Email Has Become the Bane of Our Existence

I. Hate. Email. And believe that for most of us in sales and sales management, it is our single biggest time suck. More than the sheer number of hours we spend simply managing email, what's truly maddening is how this well-intended tool, which had the potential to make us supremely productive, has accomplished the opposite. Worse, it has become a vehicle through which others can create work for us, work that often takes us away from our highest-value activities. Argh.

I'm not a life coach or a productivity guru; I just observe a lot of frontline sellers and managers and take note of what works for them and what doesn't. When it comes to email, there is a giant chasm between how the most productive people handle it and how everyone else does. Ready for this life-altering secret? Brace yourself for this highly sophisticated #SalesTruth:

Highly productive salespeople and managers decide when to check email.

Along with my anecdotal observations, I began digging to see what various productivity experts were writing regarding email management and its effect on performance and productivity. I found this gem from Rob on the *Making It Anywhere* blog that I used with a particular sales team whose company culture basically had them tethered to their inboxes: "I mean, did people in the 1960s spend all day walking to their mailbox every five minutes 'just in case'?"

As absurd as the image of interrupting ourselves and getting up from our desk to walk to the company mailroom every five minutes seems, isn't that exactly how many of us behave when it comes to checking our email? You are smiling, because for 90 percent of you reading or listening to this right now, that describes you and your addiction to your inbox. Listen, the first step to overcoming a problem is admitting you have one. Let me be first in the transparency line here: My name is Mike Weinberg, and I have a problem. I am a recovering email addict and am embarrassed to say how little control I've had over this issue for years.

It's not just that we are constantly in our inboxes; it's that we allow email to control us. Whether it is rolling over at 5:30 in the morning and grabbing our phone to see what came in overnight before even getting up to pee, getting buzzed while in an important meeting that requires our full focus, or sitting with someone we love but we can't focus because we're obsessing, wondering if someone sent something that might require a reply. We are a mess.

Remember, I'm not writing this book to help you clean up your life or improve relationships at home. My sole concern is your performance as a salesperson or sales leader, and I see lost sellers and overwhelmed managers flailing and failing every day, because they are hostages to their inbox. Many are not doing the things they must to drive results because they can't get to them. It's pathetic.

Whitson Gordon at Lifehacker said it beautifully: "Answering your email every time you see that little popup, hear that little ding, or watch that icon badge climb up another point will kill your productivity . . . and don't check it first thing in the morning or you'll never get anything done!"

There are plenty of resources where you can seek help for your email problem and many great hacks and tools that might hit the spot for you. But there is one very simple tip that works remarkably well: Schedule your inbox time. Instead of living in a state of perpetual email checking, choose set times throughout the day to retrieve and process email. Stop living in fear that you will miss something. Trust me, you want to miss more things! If there is a true emergency or something that absolutely, positively requires your involvement right now, whoever needs you will pick up the phone to either text or call you.

There are no prizes for maintaining a clean inbox, and no one is making President's Club or breaking sales records because they return emails in record time. Stop looking at email as soon as you wake up and letting others dictate your mood and your early morning priorities. *You* should decide those things. Turn off email notifications on your computer and phone. There is no reason to see that counter go up or get dinged or buzzed every time some joker sends you a trivial announcement. I promise that you will be amazed at how freed, empowered, and focused you feel once you break the chains enslaving you to your inbox. Similar to time blocking your highest-value activities, restrain yourself from allowing a low-value administrative task like reviewing email to consume you.

Stop Telling Customers You Are There for Their Every Need 24/7

If I haven't yet pushed you out of your comfort zone with my advice about becoming more selfishly productive, this next suggestion will likely do the trick.

If you are serious about upping your game to develop new business, then consider this strong request seriously: Please stop saying stupid things to customers, particularly new customers. Stop telling your accounts that you are "their guy" or "their gal" and that no matter what their need they should contact you. Stop positioning yourself to customers as their personal servant, or-der-taker, concierge, dedicated account service rep, errand boy, preferred estimator, and firefighter-in-chief.

I know that many of you reading this are scrunching your faces in confusion and wondering what I ate for breakfast that is mak-ing me so disagreeable. It's not what I ate that upset me. It's what I witness overly relational, overly service-minded, underperform-ing sales reps doing time and time again that causes me to shake my head.

Before going further with my plea to break out of an account service-first mindset, allow me to take you on a little trip down memory lane. I know it is easy to romanticize about the past and longingly recount the joys of yesteryear. My intention is not to do that here, but rather to provide a reminder that prior to the ex-istence of smartphones, heck, even before affordable mobile phones, our customers' needs were being met just fine by others. Back in the day, for the first third of my selling career, we didn't have cell phones with us in the field. We used payphones to "check in" a few times per day. I have fond memories of trying to find drive-up payphones where you could pull the car right along-side the phone and lean out to punch the keys much like we do at a drive-through ATM today.

If customers truly needed you, they would leave a voicemail, knowing you'd pick it up at some point that day or, at the latest, that evening. Customers also understood, however, that because you were in sales, you were typically out of the office, likely mak-ing sales calls or traveling to see customers. So, when customers needed immediate attention, they did not even think of leaving you a message. Instead, they would call customer service. Imagine that. Customer service serving as the primary contact for customers requiring service. How idyllic. And how logical.

We were never tempted to promise customers the crazy things that salespeople do today, because we had no way to deliver that level of "I'll drop whatever I'm doing so I can immediately respond to your text message" service. And, honestly, things worked a lot better. Both customers and salespeople understood that the salesperson's primary job was to sell.

Fast forward to today, and it is an entirely different ballgame. Due to technological advances, customers' expectations about response time have increased exponentially, and sellers in their desire to please have accommodated those expectations even when it ends up hurting, not helping, sales. When you compound the technology making us accessible 24/7 with the fact that many sellers have lost sight of their primary job, bad things happen.

Just because the capability exists for customers to use salespeople as their primary point of contact does not mean that is the right or smart thing to do. I completely understand that customers love the idea of being able to reach *their* sales representative any time they want. Further, I completely understand that control-freak salespeople are much more confident in their own ability to service an account than they are in the ability of someone else from their company. Additionally, it is easy to see why highly relational salespeople who are motivated to please their customers will gladly drop everything the moment a customer inquiry or issue arises. I get it. This is the "new way" of operating. We are supposed to be tethered to our phones and perpetually available to respond to a customer's beck and call.

We love to brag about being responsive and how productive we are because we're available to help customers all day, every day.

And many in sales love the feeling of being needed by their customers. They live for the chance to be the hero, meet the need, put out the fire, or even just enter the order.

It all sounds great. Except there's this little inconvenient thing called *results*, and the big bad #SalesTruth is that this hyperresponsive approach is not working. The results are not there. Fewer salespeople are hitting their quota. Many are working longer hours but accomplishing less. Living in reactive mode has become the norm. Undisciplined sellers change direction at the drop of a hat. Weaker salespeople have mastered the "I didn't hit my new-business-development goals because I was so busy dealing with customer issues" excuse. And somehow, someway, management has allowed this madness to go on.

The time has come to stop pretending. Things are not going to change for you unless you change them. We can't roll back technology. Smartphones are not going away, and I'm not advocating a return to payphones and calling cards. But we certainly can learn to set boundaries and communicate clear expectations to customers. Instead of volunteering ourselves as the first, best, and preferred point of contact for all things service, we can set up our support team to succeed. Stop the stupidity of telling customers, "Call me if you need anything, I'll get right on it," and instead sell your entire team and others in your company who will support the account.

High-producing sales killers have no trouble delineating between work and high-payoff, revenue-generating activity. They delegate as much service and administrative work as humanly possible. They're ruthless with their time because sales killers understand the game is won by maximizing selling time, which requires minimizing their involvement in everything else. That is exactly why you don't find the top sales hunters flipping burgers at the company picnic or telling customers to call them directly with every piddly little issue. Top-producing salespeople are selfish—in a good way. They're selfishly productive.

Now that we've got our heads and hearts right about creating new opportunities, taken back control of our calendar, and freed ourselves to actually do it, it's time to decide whose business we want and are committed to pursuing.

CHAPTER 9

Naming Strategic Target Accounts Is the First Step of a Successful Sales Attack

We have already established that most of the sales population lives in reactive mode, waiting for an opportunity or a service need to make itself known. When operating in reactive mode, you don't really need a target list declaring whose business you are committed to pursuing. You just get up every day and respond to what comes your way. You do the work put on your desk by others, and there's always plenty to do. Even if there are not enough good leads to chase, there are always favorite customers to overserve or emails to return.

However, it's a very different situation once you decide to become strategic about the business you want and how you will invest your time. The moment a salesperson commits to shifting from a reactive approach to a proactive approach, becoming more intentional about whose business is wanted, the very first thing needed is a target list.

When you are going hunting, the natural first question you ask is, "What are we hunting for? Who are we pursuing?"

Similarly, whenever I kick off a new engagement with an individual coaching client, within the first ten minutes of our first conversation, I ask to see the salesperson's target account list. It's that important. I can't help you sharpen your sales story, power up your prospecting, or perfect your probing and discovery without understanding whose business you are pursuing. Naming your strategic targets is a necessary first step for launching any new business development-focused sales attack.

True Sales Hunters Can Always Point to Their Target List

I have noticed a characteristic that top-producing sales hunters have in common. When asked, they can point to, or put their finger on, their target account list in a nanosecond. Whether it is in dry erase marker on a whiteboard in their office, a printed copy of a spreadsheet, or chicken scratched into a legal pad, true proactive new-business-development-focused sellers can tell you *and* show you exactly who they are pursuing right now.

There is nothing vague or nebulous about a sales hunter's target list. True hunters know exactly whose business they want, can articulate the reasons why these specific targets are on the list, and they dedicate chunks of calendar time to do nothing but pursue the targets. It's a thing of beauty to behold. It's also a stark contrast from what I observe from underperformers who typically have a hard time finding and presenting the list of accounts they are currently attacking.

I was reminded of the power of having a strategic, finite list when working with a somewhat awkward sales rep in New England a few years back. This particular salesperson was relatively new with his company and had been in his position for only eight months. I was consulting the chief executive officer on sales leadership, doing some *New Sales. Simplified.*-based training of the sales team, and occasionally coaching individual sales reps or spending a day in the field to get a feel for their needs.

To say that this particular salesperson was not the prototypical rep would be an understatement. You know the expression that people buy from people they like? Yeah, that didn't apply here. Not only was this fellow unlikable, he was socially awkward. He made people uncomfortable when he talked to them—which was especially damaging because he liked to talk. A lot. That's not the best trait for a salesperson ☺. He had unusual hobbies and loved to tell his customers about those too. He didn't dress well. His attire was outdated as was his hairstyle. From the moment I was around him, I was looking forward to not being around him anymore. You getting the picture of this guy? Pretty convinced that you would never hire this person? Me too.

Here's the rub. This guy was shooting the lights out. In a very short time with the company, he had not only built one of the healthiest pipelines on the sales team, but also closed a couple deals with significant target prospects—the type of deals that typically took six months or more to close. When I met with the CEO one day, he asked my opinion of this salesperson. I pursed my lips and shook my head not saying a word. The CEO, holding the pipeline report, looked up at me over the top of his reading glasses and then looked back down at the pipeline. Then he started naming these blue-chip accounts that had progressed to the "active opportunity" stage in Mr. Awkward's sales funnel. He took off his reading glasses, gave me a quizzical look, and asked: "What gives? Weinberg, what's your take on him?"

I continued to shake my head and finally offered, "I don't get it."

We agreed that I should visit New England to get a firsthand look at this awkward-but-overachieving rep in action. I think the CEO feared that Mr. Awkward was either bribing or blackmailing buyers at his accounts because his results just didn't match the person we were seeing. I planned my trip so it coincided with a Red Sox home game, which allowed me the treat of making my second trip to Fenway Park. Side note: there is no more beautiful, nostalgic, or better place to see a ball game. I've been to three-quarters of the Major League stadiums and none come close to Fenway.

I met Mr. Awkward for coffee near his branch, and he was very excited to tell me about the day he had put together for us. Too excited. Several times in the coffee shop, he mentioned that he could not wait to show me something back at the office. I was not exactly sure what to expect but my gut feeling was that whatever it might be, it would likely make me uncomfortable. After introducing me to the receptionist (awkwardly), the salesperson walked me into his pretty large office and with a good deal of fanfare, gestured to the far wall, excitedly asking, "What do you think?"

On that far wall was a masterpiece to behold. If Picasso had been in sales, this is what his office wall would have looked like! The *entire wall* was painted over with whiteboard paint and the salesperson used colored markers to create what appeared to be a combination of his target account list and his sales pipeline. Seeing that I was in awe of his creation, the sales rep (surprisingly) showed incredible restraint and didn't say a word as I stood there taking it all in. I was impressed with this first evidence of EQ, as he allowed me to simply gawk at this thing of sales beauty and begin to process the information.

We spent the next hour dissecting his list. As I'm known to do, I asked dozens of questions, and every question was met with a smart, strategic answer. My anxiety about having to spend the day with this salesperson waned as I realized that I was sitting with a sales savant. This guy wasn't bribing or blackmailing buyers to create all these sales opportunities. Shame on us. He had put more effort, more thinking, and more analysis into building out his personal target customer list than anyone I'd worked with in years. And while he was socially awkward and his wardrobe was desperately in need of an update, he was so completely laser-focused on exactly the right mix of strategic prospective customers and a small handful of existing customers with major upsell and cross-sell potential that he set himself up perfectly to win big.

The more time I spent with this salesperson, the more I appreciated his knowledge—not just of the market and where his company's offerings fit in, but that he had such a great feel for the needs of the specific companies he had chosen to target for new business. This seller was the epitome of "strategic" and such a pleasant contrast to the typical seller who takes his target list for granted and doesn't put in the necessary effort to ensure the accounts on the list are being targeted for sound reasons.

I love this example not just because it's a fun story to tell but because it so perfectly depicts the preeminent importance of having a smart list of target accounts. The #SalesTruth represented here is that when a salesperson working for a company with a good solution laser-locks in on the prospective customers who potentially and likely need that solution, and then works like mad to get in front of those customers, really good things happen.

. . .

Time Is the Great Equalizer, and All Accounts Are Not Created Equal

Here I am again talking about time. If you sense a running theme, I applaud you. Time is not a sexy topic. It's not new; it's not cool. It's a constant, and we all are given the exact same amount. I like to tell managers and salespeople that time is the great equalizer. We are all subject to it. It's finite. You can't make or buy more and once you use it, it's gone. Forever.

With that reality as the backdrop, let's examine why your target list can make or break you. As we've covered already, it's imperative to set aside dedicated time blocks to work on new opportunity creation. The success you achieve during these time blocks is directly tied to the quality of the target list you are pursuing. Sure, there are many other factors at play including your own sales skills, your messaging (which we'll tackle in the next chapter), and your comfort and effectiveness at prospecting and securing early-stage meetings, and so on, but it all starts with your target list.

Even the most supremely talented salespeople will not produce optimal results if they are pursuing the wrong accounts. Pause to let that premise sink in. You can be God's gift to the sales profession, from your looks to personality to business acumen. You may have the sharpest sales story and most polished probing skills. You might deliver the most powerful presentations and perfect proposals. But if you expend your time and energy pursuing the wrong targets, you will continually produce suboptimal results. Your strategic target list is that important, and it's essential that it is nailed down on the frontend of your sales attack.

I picked up a great expression from my friend Jeb Blount, author of the blockbuster multiyear bestseller, *Fanatical Prospecting*. Jeb and I were doing a webinar together and pounding the audience about the importance of time blocking their calendars and then actually executing the scheduled behavior during those time blocks. One of the attendees asked a question about how to account for all the time spent researching prospects during a prospecting block. I started to respond, and Jeb jumped in to interrupt, because I was being too gentle. I'll never forget this line that was classic Jeb: "Listen up, everybody! Researching is not prospecting. Researching is researching. Don't you dare confuse the two."

I love Jeb's point for another reason beyond the obvious one. Yes, if we've scheduled an outbound time block, then we need to be calling and emailing, not spending time researching every trivial detail about the contact we're trying to reach. There are tons of call-reluctant salespeople who will research a prospect to death before even thinking about picking up the phone. I agree—that's silly and unproductive, and that's why Jeb is so strong about not confusing research with your true outbound efforts. The additional valuable benefit that accrues to sellers who lock in the target list up front is that their direction is set. Sellers who nail this down don't end up wandering aimlessly, wondering which accounts they are supposed to pursue. To the contrary, they know with absolute certainty on which target accounts to train their sights.

I've been preaching for a long time about the need for *every* salesperson with a goal or quota to have a strategic, finite, written target list, and I've pushed salespeople to segment existing customers into categories, because all accounts are not created equal and don't all deserve the same amount of our energy and attention. Recently, in response to seeing so many sales teams confused about their target list, often due to management's neglect of this important topic, I have streamlined my coaching, using this graphic with anyone and everyone who will listen.

Growable Existing Accounts	Ideal Profile Prospects
	Dream Clients

The simple graphic represents my fantasy as a sales coach. I fantasize about how many more new sales opportunities would be created and how much more net new business would be acquired if every salesperson with a new-business-acquisition-and-revenue-growth goal had a two-column strategic target list that looked like this.

I realize that this exact framework won't work for every salesperson. Some sellers have no existing accounts assigned to them while others exclusively manage current customer relationships. In those cases, we would tweak the categories, or sections, of the list accordingly. However, for the 80-plus percent of sellers with whom I work who both manage existing relationships while also being charged to create new ones, this works swimmingly well.

Let's deal with the left half of the graphic first. That's where we list our Growable Existing Accounts. The key word there is *growable*. The reason I've become so obtuse on this topic is because of the prevalence of salespeople who manage existing customer relationships or territories defaulting to an account management or territory management mindset. They view themselves as account or territory caretakers, not as business developers. They see their primary responsibility as caring for the customers or geography entrusted to them. *Caring* is such a nice word, and I'm a fan of caring for others, but when used in this context, it makes me want to vomit. The staggering amount of New Sales not won because of caring, maintenance-minded salespeople who have lost sight of their most important job and morphed into babysitters and glorified customer service reps is horrifying. Repeating this for the *n*th time, hoping the message is sinking in:

The first, foremost, chief, and primary job of a professional salesperson is to increase sales, to grow revenue, to develop new business that, without the salesperson's effort, would not have come in.

And that is precisely why, if we are going to create more new opportunities to begin winning more new sales, we start our strategic targeting process by listing existing customers that have upside and potential for us to sell more.

If an existing customer relationship is not growable, meaning that we are getting more than the lion's share of the business and the potential to sell the customer more of what they already buy, or new things they don't yet buy, does not exist, then I question how much of a salesperson's time it warrants. Put more simply, if the account can't purchase more from us then we shouldn't be targeting it for new business. That's logical, yes?

I ask that you not read more into this than I'm writing. Please do not mistake what I am advocating as instruction to ignore, mistreat, or underserve your customers that are not growable. Nowhere did I say that. However, I am strenuously asking you to take a step back to revisit how you see your role and to evaluate whether you have been underinvesting in your most growable customers, because you've allowed your nongrowable accounts to take more of your mindshare and calendar than deserved.

The angriest I have ever seen a senior executive about this topic was two summers ago, when I was brought in by a newly appointed CEO to facilitate a two-day meeting. The CEO had already removed the previous vice president of sales and briefed me that he had inherited a complacent sales team with a heavy bias toward servicing accounts in a market that was flat. The only way to grow was to take business away from the competition, but his early perceptions were that this tenured sales force was having a difficult time adjusting and seemed unwilling to prioritize growth over territory management. His perceptions proved accurate right from the outset of the meeting.

To drive home his point, the CEO titled this meeting "The Growth Conference."

Several hours of Day One were allocated for each territory manager to present a brief business/territory "growth plan" for the second half of the year. These tenured sales reps used this opportunity to drive home their own point while squarely thumbing their noses at (more accurately, giving the finger to) the CEO. Salesperson after salesperson got up to present his plan (it was an old-school industrial company in the Rust Belt and the sales force was exclusively men), and after hearing just three of the fifteen presentations, it was clear these reps had conspired and colluded about their presentations. Instead of focusing on how they were going to grow their territory revenue, rep after rep shared that they would have to spend upward of 90 percent of their effort "maintaining their territory." Every single one of them used the terms *maintain, territory maintenance,* or *account maintenance,* and each one actually put a number to it. In all my years of reviewing sales/territory business plans, I had never seen anything like this.

After the sixth presentation, the CEO blew a gasket and articulated exactly what needed to be said. He blasted the sales team with truth they very much needed to hear and that I was salivating to reinforce the next day. Viewing your role as a territory caretaker will not drive sales growth, and overservicing existing customers is not a recipe for winning new business, despite what those who practice it want to believe. The primary reason sales were flat in this company is that the people in charge of growing revenue had made the conscious decision that they were there to "maintain" the business rather than expand it. Period. End of story.

I cannot state this any plainer. For salespeople who manage existing books of business, portfolios, territories, customers, or any other descriptor that applies, in order to intentionally focus on creating new opportunities and developing new business, there is no choice but to strictly limit your caretaker/maintenance activity and reallocate that time specifically to proactively work your list of growable accounts. That is exactly why it is imperative to put in the effort to create that list on the left-hand side of the strategic targeting graphic. Once sellers have listed those most growable accounts, they must then commit to activity focused on those named target accounts. The customers named on that target list should drive what goes on every salesperson's calendar. That's how we stop salespeople from doing the brainless "milk run" and from continuing to *visit* their favorite accounts instead of working the more challenging accounts where there is potential to develop new business.

Name the Names of Your Ideal Profile Prospects and Dream Accounts

If you are a salesperson tasked with acquiring new business by acquiring new accounts, completing the right side of the target list is as critical, possibly more so, than the left side. Here is where we decide which noncustomers' business we really want and will commit to pursuing.

I'm not a marketer, don't play one on TV, and didn't stay at a Holiday Inn Express last night. No one looks to me for marketing strategy, and I'm not even going to pretend I have expertise in this area. Yet, I have one very strong opinion about the prospective customers salespeople should be targeting for new business. This highly informed, very complex theory was formed from my dozen years as a top-producing sales hunter and from observing hundreds of other top-producing sales hunters across a myriad of industries. Brace yourself for this pearl of wisdom from your New York Public School educated author: Salespeople should intentionally target prospective accounts that look, smell, and feel like their company's best existing customers.

Blown away by that keen insight? I hope that is not the case.

When I was hunting for new business, whether selling custom plastic components, direct marketing programs, cloud-based learning management systems, or consulting services, my radically simple targeting philosophy was to find the path of least resistance. I was not looking to reinvent the wheel or gain acclaim for doing something new, different, and difficult. I wanted to win as much new business as possible as quickly as possible. The best way to do that? Understand the characteristics of your very best customers—the ones who love you, who appreciate the value you deliver and the outcomes you, your company, or solution provide. Once you grasp those key characteristics (size, location, industry vertical, business model, etc.) sketch out an *Ideal Customer Profile* to describe the types of prospects that belong on your target list.

The next key to successfully filling in the right side of the targeting graphic is to actually name the names of the specific prospective customers. Put. The. Names. On. Your. List. I cannot tell you how many times I ask a salesperson whom they're targeting right now and receive an overly general, nebulous response. Please don't tell me you are targeting all XYZ companies in your five-county or five-state territory. That's not a specific list. And don't tell me you are targeting the top architecture firms along the Eastern Seaboard. Or large banks. Or small banks. Or all the transportation departments for municipalities with populations greater than 25,000. Name. The. Names!

Specificity and clarity are critical. It's impossible to focus your attack without a crystal-clear list that names the specific accounts, and preferably the specific contacts (or, at least position types) within those accounts. I never ever, ever, ever see a new-business-development sales attack succeed when the sales team, or individual seller, is not laser-locked on a clear, finite, strategic list of named target prospects. Remember the story of the awkward sales rep in New England who was crushing his numbers because he not only created his ideal customer profile but did the heavy lifting up front to create his list? He's our example. Follow his lead. Do the research. Put in the work. Draft your list on the frontend, so you can turn your focus to hunting down the targets on your list.

Let me briefly address the Dream Clients category that appears on the bottom-right of our graphic. I'm a fan of salespeople reserving a small subset of their target prospect list for gigantic, monster accounts. No one writes more about pursuing your dream clients than Anthony Iannarino, who was kind enough to author the foreword for this book. Anthony's latest book, *Eat Their Lunch: Winning Customers Away from Your Competition,* is an absolute must read on this topic and will help you plan your dream client attack while providing the approaches and tools needed to win.

I love when salespeople have the guts to go after their competitor's biggest accounts. I applaud their bravery and willingness to engage in a high-risk battle where there's a better chance of getting bloodied than a probability of winning. By all means, go for it. Name a handful of monster accounts that you are committed to pursuing—the type of account that if acquired would change your year, possibly even the trajectory of your career. But my strongest coaching is to not put all your eggs in these few low-probability baskets. Oh, I get (and love) the potential upside. I've experienced that ecstasy myself and celebrated with others who've tasted that type of victory as well. Just be sure that while you're pursuing these dream clients that you also maintain the discipline of working all of your "normal"-sized target prospects too. It's those regular types of deals that pay your bills month in and month out. You want landing a dream account to be the icing on top of your enormous celebratory cake but should not be counting on it to make your house payment.

Seek Input and Commit to Your Finite List for a Season

Two final thoughts regarding your list. First, don't go it alone. This is way too important to handle all by yourself. Your ultimate success creating opportunities and closing new business is directly tied to the accounts named on both the left and right side of your target list. Don't be a lone ranger here. Naming your target accounts is one of the very few chances in a sales role to be highly strategic. Most of what we do day-to-day is tactical and about execution. Creating our list is where we need brainpower, and not just our own. Again, even the most gifted sellers will not win at the level they could be if they're pursuing the wrong targets.

Seek input. Talk to others in and outside your company. If you are a salesperson, schedule time with your manager, and possibly even others in your company, who can offer wisdom, experience, and perspective. And if you are a sales manager, I implore you to find the time to meet with every single salesperson who reports to you. You cannot take for granted that members of your team are targeting the right accounts. Your success as a manager is dependent on your team winning new business from the accounts they are proactively working. You want your fingerprints on their target lists and your people deserve your best thinking here, not just a cursory glance.

Second, commit to this finite list for a season. I am not telling you to cast the names in stone, but I strongly caution you about changing targeted accounts as often as you change your clothes. Impatient and inexperienced sales hunters get easily frustrated when they're not creating opportunities from targeted accounts as quickly as they'd like. The temptation is to jettison the names where progress has not been easy and replace them with new ones. Wiser, more experienced, and more successful hunters have more patience and continually remind themselves that often the best accounts are the toughest to crack. We put these target accounts on our list for good reasons. They are either growable existing customers or ideal profile prospective customers. We want their business and are convinced beyond a shadow of a doubt that we can deliver great value. Be slow to cross names off the list. In my own selling career, some of my best, largest, and most profitable clients took a very long time to acquire, and I am confident if you asked other top producers you would hear the same.

CHAPTER 10

A Compelling Message Increases Your Confidence and Effectiveness

Once you have shed your account management mindset, freed your calendar for more proactive selling time, and nailed down your list of strategic target accounts, nothing will increase your confidence and your effectiveness at winning new sales more than crafting a compelling message.

Sharpening what I call our *Sales Story* pays more dividends than you can imagine. When your sales story is spot-on selling is a completely new ballgame. A compelling, customer issue and customer outcome-focused, differentiating message changes everything, and I mean everything! Here are five of the biggest ways you benefit:

First, it gives you confidence—confidence to prospect and confidence to meet with anyone. I will talk to any business owner, senior executive, sales leader, or salesperson because I know that the first few thoughts out of my mouth will create interest, intrigue, credibility, and a willingness to dialogue. Give me between ten seconds and a minute to share my "story," and I will string together compelling and salient talking points that I know with certainty will hit the spot. When you have that level of confidence in your messaging, prospecting becomes a whole lot easier. So much so, that you actually look forward to it instead of dreading it. And the reverse is true as well. If you are not confident in your message, I don't how in the world you would muster up the courage to pick up the phone or even believe that you could be effective pursuing prospects.

Second, a powerful customer issue and customer outcome driven message gets your target contact's attention. When the lead-in to your story is about things that matter deeply to your contact, they immediately engage and begin to listen.

Third, your effective message not only gets your client's attention but also changes the entire dynamic of the buyer-seller interaction. The norm is that when a salesperson begins to speak (pitch), the buyer begins to resist. Most pitches lead with the product/service/solution. This self-focused messaging turns off customers, who immediately sense this and deploy their defense shields. It's automatic. The seller speaks or emails (a self-focused pitch), and the buyer instantly recoils, resists, and assumes a defensive posture. However, the seller with a compelling customer issue/outcome focused story gets a very different reception. Instead of getting the Heisman stiff-arm stop sign, the buyer, hearing a relevant message focused on the issues and outcomes that matter to him, indicates that he wants to hear more. That type of customer-focused messaging immediately gets sellers perceived as value-creators and professional problem solvers, as opposed to pitchmen peddling a product.

Fourth, your customer-issue-driven message warms up the buyer for your discovery effort and increases the customer's willingness to answer your probing questions. When customers hear that we are helping people in positions and businesses similar to theirs, they become more open to sharing about their own situation. A good message credentials us as experts and increases the buyer's comfort in being more transparent with us.

And fifth, a truly great sales story sets you and your company apart and helps justify your premium price. When your story is more about the customer, its needs, desires, risks, challenges, initiatives, and desired results, you become memorable. That's a very different approach than most sellers take. Buyers are intrigued that you don't sound like every other amateur seller who is either leading with his product or bragging about how great his company is.

The other critical function of your story is that it helps rationalize your pricing. When you charge more than your competition, you need words that articulate the higher level of value your solution creates. As I've written many times in many places, a premium price requires a premium story, and nothing helps justify our higher pricing better than a story that effectively describes the outcomes other customers experience buying from us.

Self-Focused Messaging Is the Most Common Sales Story Sin

Salespeople commit many sins when sharing their story, but the most common one by far is being self-focused. For reasons I do not comprehend, salespeople love to talk about their own company, and many marketing departments are aiding and abetting sellers committing this common sin. Whether it is leading the "About Us" section of the company website with a long, boring, myopic chronology of the company's history or providing PowerPoint decks stuffed with organizational charts, it sure appears that too many marketing managers are clueless about what matters to customers. And salespeople, particularly newer or weaker

SALES TRUTH

salespeople who don't know any better, follow the horrible lead from marketing and actually use this boring, irrelevant, self-absorbed drivel as part of their messaging.

Slightly more advanced sellers progress from talking company history to making the feature set of their product the focus of their story. What's amusing is that in spite of the universal acceptance that leading with your product is an awful sales approach destined to get you, at best, commoditized, and at worst, ignored, so many salespeople are obsessed with their own products and infatuated with talking about feature sets. This happens with salespeople selling everything from big data to big equipment and from plastics to payroll services. It doesn't matter whether they're demoing a slick software solution or a Class 8 truck, the focus of the message is still the same and still pathetic. Feature. Feature. Feature. Feature. It does this. It does that. Blah, blah, blah, blah, blah.

Try This Low-Pressure-Scenario Sales Story Test

When facilitating workshops with sales teams, I like to test participants with an exercise that forces them to tell their story in a low-pressure scenario before we dive deep into a more comprehensive exercise to sharpen their messaging.

Here's the scenario I share, and I'd like for you to do this exercise now before reading ahead. You and your neighbor are on the way to a social event. It could be a tailgate party before a big football game, the neighborhood July 4 barbeque, some event at your kids' school. Pick whichever scenario is more likely to fit you or adapt it to something more realistic where you might be headed with a neighbor or good friend. I'll use the tailgate party to set up the exercise.

You're in the car with your neighbor driving to the stadium, and he excitedly tells you that Joe Wilson from ABC Corporation is going to be at the tailgate party before the game. Joe Wilson just happens to be your perfect contact (the exact right director or executive) at one of the dream clients you listed on your target list. You are thrilled and thank your neighbor for the heads-up. Joe Wilson is someone you would love to meet, but haven't yet had the chance. Your neighbor knows Joe through a mutual friend and is looking forward to introducing you. As you and your neighbor are walking toward the parking spots where Joe is tailgating, you sense that everyone is in a festive mood and the vibe is super positive. Your neighbor immediately spots Joe, shakes his hand, and brings him over to you. Joe is smiling ear to ear, appears to have already enjoyed several beers, and has just a touch of mustard on his cheek from the bratwurst he's eating.

Your neighbor says: "You two need to meet. Joe, this my neighbor [Your Name], and he's with [Your Company Name]."

Joe smiles even bigger and greets you warmly. "Nice to meet you. I've heard of [Your Company]. Now, remind me exactly what it is you do and tell me what you're up to these days."

So, you are in this safe, fun, low-pressure environment, and the perfect contact at a dream prospect account is as happy as could be and asks what you do and what your company is up to. I am giving you thirty to forty-five seconds to answer Joe. What will you say to entice him enough to invite you to his office for a follow-up meeting? Take some time now to sketch out a handful of talking points and really think through how you would respond. Oh yes, one more thing. I know because you're a total professional that your sales gut is telling you that instead of sharing your story with Joe you should turn it around and ask him a few questions. I applaud your sales instinct to create a dialogue and begin probing, but that is not the point of this exercise. So subjugate your instinct and play along with my request. Go ahead and craft five or so points to share with Joe.

I so badly wish I could hear the responses you prepared, because it would lead to a healthy debate on what we could, or should, be saying in that situation. I learn something every time I lead this exercise, but unfortunately, I am also usually disappointed by the lackluster points salespeople list as their response to this all-so-important prospect. Here is a smattering of genericized sample talking points that salespeople typically share:

- "We provide [fill in the blank]."
- "We are the largest DEF company in our space."
- "We manufacture/supply [fill in the blank]."
- "We've been in business forty-seven years."
- "We are privately held."
- "Our unique processes [fill in the blank]."

What's wrong with each of these talking points? In and of themselves, nothing, but as the lead-in to your sales story, a whole lot is wrong. What's the focus of every one of those points? Exactly! They are either about the company or the offering. There is nothing in it for the potential customer. *Nothing.* Zero reason for this dream prospect to pay attention and definitely nothing articulated that might cause him to invite you in for a meeting.

I have been brought in several times to train sales reps at a large, proud, American company that manufactures heavy duty trucks. They've been in business for more than a hundred years and have a truly iconic brand. Many of the dealerships they sell through have been representing this manufacturer for decades and decades. Understandably, these dealers are very proud of their long history selling these trucks. However, sometimes pride and long tenure can actually hinder, rather than increase, sales effectiveness. These dealer sales reps have been selling this brand for so long that many have lost sight of what matters to the customer and they sell from a myopic mindset. When I lead this same low-pressure scenario exercise with dealer sales reps, even after pointing out the pitfalls of leading your story by talking about your company and your product, they still rattle off some version of these self-focused points a surprising amount of the time:

> *Our dealership is a fourth-generation, family-owned business, and I've been with the company since 1992. We have fourteen locations. Every [Brand] Truck we sell today has a serial number that starts with the number "1," and every [Brand] Truck we have ever sold had a serial number that began with a "1." That's because these trucks have always been made right here in the US of A.*

Honestly, I love the pride. I respect the heritage of the brand. I admire these dealers who are all-in for this manufacturer. I am in awe of the health and strength of dealers who have succeeded from generation to new generation. I have nothing but good feelings toward these dealers, many of whom have engaged me directly to help their sales teams or sales managers. But when I hear their salespeople regurgitating these tired, self-absorbed story talking points, I am compelled to scream at them:

> *Customers do NOT care what you do, how much you love your company or your product, or how long you've been in business. They want to know what is in it for them.*

I continue the sermon, getting louder and angrier with each sentence:

> *I have driven exactly one heavy-duty truck in my life, and that was on the test track at your factory. I know practically nothing about*

trucks and the truck business. But this much I do know: The biggest issues on your customers' minds are driver recruitment and retention, fuel economy, uptime, and total cost of ownership. I only know this because every time I am at a big meeting, [Brand] shares that critical information with you. All the industry data says the same thing. So if those four big things are top of mind for every customer, why in the world do you insist on going in and talking about how long your freaking dealership has been in business and bragging for the umpteenth time that [Brand] Trucks are made in America?!?!

As you are processing my rant, please resist the temptation to chalk this up to the fact that these were just *truck salesmen,* and that people in your industry are more sophisticated and would never go into an account leading with company history. I promise you, many supposedly sophisticated sellers are doing exactly that and worse. Even the very highly educated (as in masters or doctorate degrees in engineering) business development managers at my most complex, sophisticated client (a defense company) regularly open presentations by showing organization charts, as if any customer in the entire history of mankind was sitting around just hoping that a supplier would come in and present an org chart! So before dismissing this sales story sin as being beneath you, I would ask that you take a long look in the mirror, or better yet, at your outbound emails, prospecting call talking points, voicemail outlines, and first few presentation deck slides.

Never Ever Answer This Question, at Least the Way It Is Asked

Now that you've completed the low-pressure exercise, rolled your eyes at my rant, and reviewed the story-lead in many of the key sales tools that "carry" your message, let me offer some pointed coaching.

In sales, we are often asked a seemingly innocent question that I strongly recommend we never answer—or at least not answer it the way it was asked. It's pretty common for someone to ask us any variation of this question:

"What do you do?" or "What is it that your company does?"

Looking back to the low-pressure story exercise, that is pretty much what Joe Wilson asked you at the tailgate party. And Joe, like others who ask that innocently, was sincere in his desire to hear the answer. People don't ask us that to trick us. They want to know. The problem, however, is a huge one. Stated simply, if you provide the answer to any variation of that question, you will undoubtedly end up talking about what it is that you or your company do, and truthfully, that doesn't help us. The harsh reality is that buyers don't give a flip about what you do. What they really want to know is what you can do for them! Repeating that point with a slightly different twist: From the customer's perspective, it does not matter what we do. They could not care less about our "offerings" (products and services). They want to know what we (and our solutions) will achieve for them. Subtle? Yes, very. But incredibly significant.

As you picked up in chapter 4, I'm not a fan of politicians and don't typically hold them out as role models we should follow. But in this particular case, we can learn a ton from how they handle questions. The one area where skilled politicians continually impress is in their ability to deftly answer a different question than the one they're asked. Have you noticed how rare it is to get a succinct, straight answer from a politician who gets asked a perfectly straightforward question? I don't believe they're always trying to avoid the question they're asked, but rather that they are so intentionally focused on communicating a particular message to their target audience. And delivering an on-target, compelling, constituent (client/prospect) focused message is something that sellers must become very adept at doing.

Power-Up Your Story by Shifting from Self-Focused to Outcome-Focused Messaging

There are two keys to powering-up your sales story. First, we stop saying and writing the lazy, thoughtless, easy, weak, self-focused drivel that just about every salesperson uses. Just stop. Full stop. Cold turkey. Pull a Roberto Duran, put your hands up, and say, "no mas." The second key is to, instead, alter our messaging to begin with the OUTCOMES we produce for our customers.

For many in sales, that means radically changing the legacy way you've been prospecting, presenting, and proposing. No more pictures of buildings in presentation decks. Unless you work for an architecture firm or a resort, no one needs to see your building. You should lose your sales license for even once showing a picture of your building in a sales situation. And if your egotistical owner or clueless marketing person pushes back and thinks you're crazy for not including pretty pictures of their beloved facility, please give them my phone number and I'll show them crazy.

No more capabilities lists. No more demo-first feature dumps. No more leading with how long your company has been in business or what generation of family ownership it is in. No more thumbing through brochures or dumping samples on the table to start a sales call. No more beginning prospecting calls, voicemails, or emails with, "We are a (fill in the blank) and we (manufacture/produce/distribute, etc.)."

Nothing will make your messaging more powerful than trading out the self-focused language for customer-focused language. Replace the we are and the we do verbiage with outcome-driven talking points. Powering-up our story requires quickly getting to the issues that are top of mind for customers. Your customers and prospective customers have problems to be solved, pain they would like removed. They want liabilities reduced, risks mitigated, shortcomings overcome, and they desire to experience new and improved results. All of those are OUTCOMES. Think about how differently you and your message would be received if the very first things the customer heard or read from you were about issues that mattered deeply to them.

One of the most popular chapters in my book, *New Sales. Simplified.*, is chapter 8—"Sharpening Your Sales Story." There I list the three essential ingredients for drafting a compelling, customer-issue-focused, and differentiating story:

1. The Issues You Address for Customers (outcomes you achieve)
2. Your Offerings
3. Differentiators (that set apart you, your company, and your offering)

After having now personally helped sharpen hundreds of sales stories since that book's release, I am convinced that even more important than those three ingredients for creating a powerful story, is how critical it is to quickly articulate those customer issues and outcomes. Good things happen when we engage the customer's heart and mind by leading with issues they care about, and bad things happen when we don't. It's that simple.

The challenge, however, is that it is not natural to lead with customer issues and outcomes. We don't typically speak or write that way. Revisiting Joe Wilson and his tailgate party question again, he did not inquire about what your company could achieve for him. He asked what your company did. The natural easy response is to answer that question. And when we are prospecting or kicking off a discovery meeting (early stage sales call), the natural and easy thing to do is start telling the prospect about your company and your solutions.

If someone asks me what I do or requests that I tell them about my business, the easy, lazy, reflex response is to simply answer the question. "I'm a consultant, coach, speaker and author. I consult executives, coach sales leaders and salespeople, lead sales training workshops, and I've authored three books." And while that was smooth and sounds nice, not only is it self-focused and all about me, it is not compelling in any way, shape, or form. Unless the person who asked me was looking for someone with those specific offerings at that very moment, that message falls flat. Who cares that I train salespeople or write books? So what?

But what if instead of listing my *offerings,* I pivoted the response to focus on issues I address for my clients and the outcomes I help produce? How different and more powerful would my story be then? "Senior executives look to me when they've had it with their sales team living in reactive mode and either missing out on opportunities completely, or arriving late and being perceived as commodity sellers having to compete on price. I help their salespeople become masters at creating new opportunities, keeping the pipeline healthy and full, and closing more New Sales."

Don't blow by the contrast between those two versions of my story. Could they be more different in their impact? It's night and day. How much more confident and effective would you be developing new opportunities if you could conversationally rattle off relevant, compelling points that succinctly articulate the value your company/solution delivers? And imagine if you had various sets of talking points from which you could select the most relevant ones to use, depending on what you know about a particular prospect or customer.

Use This "Bridge Line" to Bridge into Your Message

It is pretty rare for someone to come right out and ask us what issues we address for customers and what type of outcomes our solution creates. Further, as we already reviewed, it is easier and more natural to simply begin our story by sharing information about ourselves, our company, and our solutions. That is why the majority of sellers succumb to this inferior practice. It doesn't take any extra effort. But it takes intentionality to break out of that mold and to break the habit of leading with self-focused messaging.

We need a mechanism to force us out of the legacy way of sharing our story and "bridge" us into talking about the issues we address and outcomes we achieve for customers. That is why I created what I call "The Bridge Line."

The Bridge Line forcefully prevents us from leading with our offerings or self-focused messaging and instead propels us into listing customer issues and outcomes. In my own story example above, you can see how that first sentence stops me from answering the "What do you do?" question the easy way and instead helps me bridge right into the challenges I help sales leaders and sales teams overcome and the results/outcomes I produce. This one little, very powerful line accomplishes all of that: *"Senior executives look to me when . . ."* From there, I transition into listing the handful of client issues I address that I feel are most relevant for the particular person with whom I am speaking.

When helping salespeople and sales teams sharpen their story, I promise them that if they start their messaging with any variation of The Bridge Lines below, whatever they say or write next will be good—and powerful.

[Customer Type] turns to [Your Company Name] when/to . . .

or

[Position Type] looks to [Your Solution] when/to . . .

Try it for yourself. Plug in either the type of customer or the position of the person with whom you would be sharing your story.

Here's an example to help. Assume you sold financing programs to individual orthodontists and larger orthodontic practices, so they could offer patients long-term financing to pay for braces. You might start your messaging with any of these Bridge Lines:

"Orthodontic practices turn to JKL Credit Services when . . ."

or

"Practice Business Managers look to JKL Credit when . . ."

or, this more commonly used phrase that incorporates help

"JKL Credit Services helps Orthodontics Practices who . . ."

Once we have laid down that bridge, the fun begins. Now we bridge into a select handful of talking points that articulate the true value we deliver by listing the issues we address and the outcomes we help clients achieve. The situation and communication vehicle dictate how many of those points we might initially share. During a prospecting call, I might only share two, maybe three short points—taking only ten to fifteen seconds to do that. To position my company and build credibility before asking probing questions during a discovery meeting, I might take two whole minutes to run through a longer list of issues and outcomes. When manning a trade show booth, I might be prepared to quickly rattle off four ways we are helping clients improve results.

Regardless of the situation, how long the interaction, or how many compelling points we deploy, the bottom line is that leading with customer issues addressed and customer outcomes achieved is exponentially more powerful than describing your company history, organizational structure, or product's features.

Salespeople Need Customer Success Stories and Case Studies

For all the talk about the importance of crafting case studies, it is rare to see a company invest the appropriate effort to arm the sales team with them. What would be a more powerful weapon in a seller's hand than the ability to make the connection between a customer or prospect's current situation (need or desired outcome) and a relevant success story where the company helped a customer who was in a similar situation? Salespeople not only need great case studies, but they must become what I call *conversationally comfortable* deploying them.

Occasionally I'll be working with a rookie salesperson or seasoned seller who is new with their company, and I ask how comfortable they are sharing the company story. They often respond that they are not comfortable at all. They are not yet sure what to talk about with potential customers, and they don't have enough firsthand exposure to customer success stories. To me, this is completely unacceptable. Salespeople must be armed with a range of case studies that cover the gamut of their company's offerings and the types of situations where those offerings apply. And let's not get wigged-out by the term "case studies." That is just a fancy way of saying customer success stories. It shouldn't take an act of Congress to create a handful of one-page success stories and teach them to the sales team. Frankly, I don't know how in the world a company could expect salespeople to succeed, especially newer salespeople, if they are not able to easily, quickly, and *conversationally comfortably* share examples of how their company has helped customers in similar situations. Those are table stakes if there's any hope of succeeding.

A solid, usable case study has three very simple components:

- The customer's situation when we found them or became engaged
- What we did
- The outcome

It doesn't get much simpler and that is why I go nuts when large, bureaucratic organizations make it seem like it's too hard to create case studies for the sales team. Large companies with insecure or overly involved marketing departments, or overburdened sales executives, tend to make the process of drafting case studies much more complex and laborious than it needs to be. When I spearhead this exercise, I gather the sales team in a room and have everyone list what they believe are their best, strongest, most dramatic customer success stories. We then have sellers quickly share the stories they are suggesting to the group and decide which are the most compelling. We also work to ensure that the stories chosen to be drafted are diverse enough to cover the variety of potential customer situations and that these stories represent a healthy assortment of their company's offerings. From there, we assign small teams of sellers to work together drafting very brief (less than one page) case studies that follow the simple template:

The Customer's Situation → What We Did → The Outcome

Before I go any further outlining the final phases of this case study exercise, let me address the risk averse or legalistic reader shaking his head and frowning on my ubersimple approach to drafting these success stories. I hear you. I thoroughly comprehend that this methodology would not work in a highly regulated industry (like pharmaceuticals) or in an environment where data must be precise and verifiable. I fully realize, too, that in many cases, it would not be appropriate to share the name or even too many specifics about another client's situation or results. By no means am I encouraging anyone to break the law, violate industry norms, or betray a client's confidential information. But in 90 percent of the businesses I am in, this process works great and salespeople are thrilled to have the help. The point I'm trying to make is that it should not be a nine-month project to arm the sales team with compelling case studies. On multiple occasions, I have personally spearheaded this type of initiative, and in a matter of weeks, successfully put a dozen customer success stories into my client's salespeople's hands.

Once the case studies are drafted, they are reviewed for accuracy, edited for clarity, and distributed to the sales team. But it's not enough for a salesperson to *have* these studies in writing. They must be committed to memory, and I cannot think of a more worthwhile investment of time and brainpower than for sellers to study and memorize these customer success stories. Salespeople need to be so familiar with these client situations, what their company did to address these situations, and the accompanying outcomes, that the moment they hear of a prospective client with a similar situation, they are able to draw on that specific case study and incorporate the story naturally into conversation.

How much more confident and effective would salespeople be when it comes to creating new sales opportunities if they are armed with a compelling, customer-issue-and-outcome-focused message and case studies that reinforce this messaging?

• CHAPTER 11 •

Prospecting
Is Not Optional

All the advice offered in the past four chapters amounts to absolutely nothing if sellers don't commit to personally, proactively pursuing prospective customers! They can have the purest motivation, best attitude, cleanest calendar, most strategic target list, and sharpest messaging, but if they don't actually execute the behaviors that create new opportunities at the top of the funnel, nothing changes. Nothing.

I am writing this chapter about prospecting as I sit in the office of the National Strategic Selling Institute in Manhattan. No, not that Manhattan. The other one. The nicer one. Manhattan, Kansas, of course—the place affectionately known as "The Little Apple," voted one of the best college towns in America, and the home of Kansas State University, which is perennially ranked by Princeton Review as a top ten university in multiple categories, including happiest students, quality of life, and students who love their college. I admit that I have fallen in love with K-State too.

Five years ago, Dr. Dawn Deeter, distinguished chair of the National Strategic Selling Institute, and I struck up a friendship.

She had recently joined the faculty at Kansas State to spearhead a new professional selling program and had begun using *New Sales. Simplified.* as a textbook in her Advanced Sales class. I've been blessed to guest-teach a session of that class each spring, build relationships with students in the program, and follow the success many are having very early in their careers. I'm in Manhattan to guest teach a 500-level sales leadership class for the fabulous Dr. Michael Krush, who joined Kansas State this fall and has his students reading *Sales Management. Simplified.* as part of the course.

It has been exciting to watch the K-State Sales Program blossom the past few years. The National Strategic Selling Institute is thriving. More students than ever are enrolled in the program. Professional Selling just became an official major within the college of business at the university, and dozens of companies are actively recruiting students out of the program. Oh, how I wish more universities would offer this type of undergraduate program. The sales community would benefit tremendously.

You might be wondering what my presence in Manhattan, Kansas, on a snowy November day has to do with a chapter on prospecting for new business. It has everything to do with it because this program is preparing students to succeed in sales careers not only by teaching them how to prospect, but by actually making them do it.

After teaching the sales leadership class, I met with Dr. Deeter and Dr. Krush and asked what type of feedback they were receiving from companies who had hired graduates of the sales program. Their response affirmed my gut feeling. Managers at these companies were raving about the fact that these students came to their sales teams with real prospecting experience. Unlike many new hires, these Kansas State sales graduates were comfortable picking up the phone because they had done it time and time again as students in the program. Hiring managers continue stressing to Dr. Deeter the importance of new sellers being able to effectively prospect to generate appointments and initiate sales conversations. Their biggest frustrations are with salespeople who struggle to incorporate outbound calling into their sales attack and are reluctant to prospect.

In spite of the populist belief that the telephone is no longer en vogue, and all the derogatory things declared by today's supposed sales experts, the telephone remains an incredibly effective vehicle to deliver your message and to secure a meeting with a prospective customer.

In the introduction I provided for Mark Hunter's brilliant and practical book, *High-Profit Prospecting: Powerful Strategies to Find the Best Leads and Drive Breakthrough Sales Results*, I confidently proclaimed that if readers implement the approaches and techniques in the book, their pipelines will get fatter and healthier and their sales are going to increase. Why was I able to state this so plainly? Because there's a little secret that every top producer in sales knows, and it's the same secret that Mark knows. Top producers take full responsibility for the health of their own pipelines by creating their own sales opportunities, and they demonstrate this commitment by prospecting All. The. Time.

Mark, in his book, does a masterful job at dispelling many common myths about prospecting and he obliterates one of the most dangerous misconceptions by debunking what he calls Myth #2, "I'll prospect when I'm done taking care of my existing customers." You, I, and anyone with any real-world sales experience knows that it doesn't work that way. Nobody prospects after servicing existing customers. When prospecting is not a priority and not intentionally scheduled, it doesn't happen. No salesperson I've encountered discovers a few free minutes at the end of busy and exhausting day and exclaims, "Oh wonderful, I've serviced all my existing accounts—let me spend this last half-hour phoning prospects." True sales hunters prioritize prospecting. It's never an afterthought; it's their first thought and the first high-value activity blocked in the calendar!

Don't Make Prospecting Something That It Is Not

Part of the reason that so many people dread prospecting or fear making the proactive phone call is because, in their minds, they turn it into something much bigger, much harder, much more complex than it needs to be.

You will notice that I don't refer to a prospecting phone call as a cold call. The term cold call has been so misused and abused, and creates such a powerful, often emotional response, that I find it helps to replace the word cold with the word proactive.

Proactively picking up the phone to call a potential customer is not dirty. It's not inappropriate. It's not unethical or illegal. And it's not below even the most successful salespeople—many of whom earn hundreds of thousands of dollars, or even millions, per year. There is nothing wrong with using the phone. It's not an antiquated approach, and for that matter, neither is knocking on doors! Are you aware that respected major corporations still deploy in-person prospecting as a primary means of developing new business? And I'm not just talking about Girl Scouts selling cookies. I am referring to highly respected, award-winning companies. Companies like Edward Jones, a firm that manages over one trillion dollars of assets and is a perennial top five winner of *Fortune* magazine's Best Companies to Work For. Jones has its financial advisors out pounding the streets and knocking on doors in neighborhoods surrounding their offices. Ram Tool Construction Supply is the company with the single healthiest culture I have worked with in the past few years and its sales force prospects for new business by driving their white pickup trucks onto construction jobsites and popping in (briefly and respectfully) to call on superintendents and contractors. Comcast's Xfinity sales reps sell cable television and internet services to lapsed customers going door-to-door. All three companies' sales teams are outrageously successful at bringing in new business via in-person prospecting. Prospecting is not a last resort for these respected sales organizations; it's a primary and required element of their new business development sales process.

On the other hand, the salespeople who struggle with proactive calling tend to make prospecting into something bigger, scarier, and more difficult than it actually is. Whether it's bad tapes playing in their minds that create negative emotions and the belief that prospecting is below them, or it's just simple fear that paralyzes them, those who are inexperienced at proactively calling prospects lack a vision for what successful prospecting looks like.

Simplify the Prospecting Call

Let's demystify the proactive call. I have found that it really helps salespeople new to (or scared of) prospecting to break it down into its simplest elements. Below is the flow of a typical call attempt with a touch of coaching sprinkled in:

- You initiate contact with the prospect
- You reach your intended contact (or a gatekeeper, or voicemail, both of which we'll address shortly)
- You say hello and speak in a normal, authentic manner
- Knowing that the prospect was not expecting your call

and that you are likely interrupting them, you acknowledge that interruption, say something that builds credibility, and then express the reason for your call (that you
believe you can help them)

- The prospect either resists, asks a clarifying question, or
  expresses interest
- You respond appropriately, tease the contact with a value
  nugget (an outcome you achieve) from your sales story,
  and then ask the prospect for a meeting
- The prospect typically rejects your initial request
- You ask again for the meeting, offer more value and more
  reasons (outcomes) why it would be a good decision for
  the prospect to meet with you
- The prospect either agrees to meet with you or rebuffs
  you again. If they agree to a meeting then schedule it, or
  ask yet one more time for the meeting making it clear
  that the prospect will get significant value and ideas from
  the time invested, even if there is no next step for you
- The prospect accepts your third request and you schedule the meeting

There is nothing complex or mystical about conversation flow
just outlined. Even better, there are no physical risks to the seller
attempting prospecting calls. As far as I'm aware, no one has ever
been injured while phoning a prospective customer! Further,
there are no tricks, secret code words, or special tools required.

I have personally executed this outline thousands of times myself, and I have helped thousands of other salespeople master the
very same approach. It works. And it works especially well when
executed well.

Others will argue that contacting someone who is not expecting your call is not as effective or as efficient as calling a warm

lead who has already expressed some type of interest. I agree. Others preach that referral selling produces a higher yield and that we are much more likely to have a productive conversation with someone to whom we've been referred. I agree with that too. Who doesn't love a solid lead or a powerful referral? We should absolutely work to garner as many qualified leads as possible and seek referrals from anyone and everyone who can increase our credibility and introduce us to prospective customers. But the reality in just about every sales situation I've encountered is that there are not enough leads and referrals to sufficiently fill the top of the sales funnel regardless of how strong the inbound marketing effort or well-crafted and disciplined the referral requests. That is exactly why I tell anyone who will listen that prospecting is not optional, and that it's the reason top-producing sales hunters perpetually prospect.

Chapter 9 of *New Sales. Simplified.* provides a comprehensive guide for making outbound prospecting calls. For the past six years I've been teaching that material and then observing sellers implementing my keys to proactive calling. The salespeople having the most success converting prospecting activity into sales opportunities stand out from the crowd because they have clearly mastered the following basics:

- They believe with absolute certainty that they will succeed at securing meetings with target prospects
- They anticipate resistance from the prospect and are mentally and emotionally prepared to respond appropriately
- They understand that you actually can start building a relationship with someone who has yet to respond to your calls and emails, and they earn a callback with perseverance and creativity

We covered the importance of having the right mindset and truly believing that personal prospecting will create new opportunities in chapter 7. Let's look at these two other critical keys that, when mastered, will drastically increase the number of meetings you secure with target prospects.

Anticipate Resistance and Prepare to Respond

I have bad news for you. In the overwhelming majority of cases, regardless of how great you sound, how compelling your messaging, and how strongly you believe that proactive calling will result in securing that discovery meeting you so badly want, the prospect will likely decline your first request for a meeting. But, worry not. You are not even close to done yet.

Buyers resist salespeople, especially uninvited salespeople who interrupt them. And let's not sugarcoat it. That is exactly what a proactive call is—an interruption. The fact is that very few of your prospects are bored, underworked, and sitting around just hoping an unfamiliar salesperson will call to request a meeting. Unless you hit the jackpot by calling a prospect on the exact day that the thing you sell broke, or the boss just charged your contact with upgrading their existing solution, the odds are low that your initial request for a meeting will receive an enthusiastic yes! Contrary to George Costanza's maxim in the infamous *Seinfeld* "Phone Message" episode, in which George proclaims that if he doesn't get an enthusiastic yes when asking a woman out then he's "outta there," I strongly suggest you hang in there and ask again.

In all my years prospecting, I can barely recall more than a handful of instances where the prospect accepted my first ask to meet. The good news is that I was able to secure hundreds upon hundreds of meetings after hearing that first no. The key to securing all of those meetings? No does not always mean no in sales! We must take the legendary Jim Rohn's advice to heart and bounce off that first no. Rohn, often credited as the father of the self-improvement movement, influenced and mentored many greats, including Jack Canfield, Tony Robbins, and Brian Tracy. One of his most famous quotes is that "Salespeople should take lessons from their kids. What does the word 'no' mean to a kid? Almost nothing." And when we are prospecting, that is exactly what it should mean to us. Nothing.

That first no is automatic. It doesn't mean you did anything wrong. It doesn't mean that this is not a good prospect for you. It doesn't even mean that now is not the right time for this specific prospect. It only means one thing: You asked for the meeting once and you received the standard, automatic response. This exact point in the proactive call is where we begin to separate those who are truly committed to creating their own new sales opportunities and know what to do, from those who aren't committed or don't know how to navigate past no.

Several years ago, I was coaching a bright, likeable, driven, young salesperson living in Asia. We would meet via Skype video every ten days. This up and coming young salesperson was experiencing solid results and was looking to up his new business development game. We had worked through his strategic target list and spent significant time sharpening his story/messaging. We were just beginning to review the Keys to Proactive Calling when he shared that he was planning a business trip back to his home country in Europe. Due to the high cost of this trip, his company was understandably pressuring him to maximize the number of meetings with potential accounts in his home country. He shared with me that he was not booking appointments as quickly as he would have liked despite making a high volume of outbound calls.

I had the salesperson review for me the flow of his proactive call and was impressed with everything from his voice tone, to his mini-message, to how he went about asking for the meeting. Everything sounded great all the way through the point of requesting the meeting. He was even using one of my favorite words by telling prospects that he would love the opportunity to *visit* with them to learn more about their situation and share how he had been helping similar companies experience dramatically improved results. It was all perfect except for what came next. The salesperson was not expecting to be told no after doing such a wonderful job early on during the prospecting call, and because he was such a relational and respectful fellow, he was not comfortable pushing back after hearing that first no. In fact, he was so nice that after having his initial request rejected, he would ask the prospect's permission to keep them on his list and if it would be okay to try them again in six months.

After relaying his approach, the salesperson paused as he saw me smiling big on his computer screen from 8,000 miles away. I affirmed how well he was handling the early part of the call and then asked if would be willing to step out of his natural comfort zone during his prospecting calls if it meant producing 10x the number of meetings? You can predict his response and we began working to help overcome his own reflexive desire to acquiesce at the first sign of resistance.

Please hear me on this. I am not advocating that we should be pushy, belligerent, conflict-seeking sellers. By no means. However, this is one of the very few places in the entire sales process that we truly must stand our ground and push back against resistance. The highly relational conflict-averse seller who turns tail after hearing that first no when requesting a meeting is going to struggle mightily to create new opportunities. For some of us, this is easy-peasy. We are not even fazed by resistance; we push right by it, and don't think twice about minor conflict. Others, however, freeze or freak at the first hint of potential conflict. If that is you, I want to challenge you to allow yourself to be uncomfortable for twenty seconds at this phase of a proactive call. That is the exact coaching conversation I had with the salesperson in Asia. The moment he committed to overcoming his natural tendency to acquiesce, everything improved for him. I didn't ask him to change his style or his tone, or even his verbiage. I simply asked him not to cave in after hearing that first no and to prepare to ask a second and then a third time for the meeting.

Sell the Meeting Not Your Solution

The first key to securing more meetings is anticipating the resistance and being prepared and willing to bounce off the no to ask again. Plain and simple. The salesperson who hears that first no, apologizes for interrupting, and then thanks prospects for their time is going to starve. The second key to more effective proactive calling is equally important. We must avoid the temptation to start pitching our wonderful solution in response to our initial meeting request being rejected.

One of the biggest mistakes prospecting is when salespeople try to overcome the rejection (or objection) from the buyer by pivoting away from asking for the meeting to selling their product/service. Many (mistakenly) believe that if they launch into a powerful pitch detailing all the wonderful attributes of their offering then buyers will be convinced to change their minds and invite the salesperson in for a meeting. In reality, the reverse happens and that approach backfires. Pivoting from asking for the meeting to pitching your wares only helps the prospect come up with more specific objections as to why they should not meet with you.

During a proactive call it is imperative that we keep our primary objective front and center. We. Want. The. Meeting. We are not calling the phonebook or being fed random calls from an autodialer. These prospects are on our list for good strategic reasons. The primary objective of our proactive call, whether by phone or even when doing pop-in prospecting, is to secure that discovery meeting—not to qualify the prospect, not to pitch our product. Unless you are an inside salesperson selling a more transactional, short sales-cycle solution and your job is to make the sale by phone, we must laser focus on securing the meeting. So my strongest coaching is to Sell. The. Meeting!

When you face resistance, don't start selling your solution. Sell the value the prospect will receive from spending just a little bit of time with you. Let the prospect know that along with learning more about their situation, you'll share how you are helping other people like them or organizations like theirs. Make it abundantly clear that whether or not there ends up being a fit, your prospect will leave that discovery meeting challenged by what you share and with fresh perspective, ideas, and insights. The mindset I coach sellers to adopt is that we should go into this proactive call believing that the prospect would have to be a fool to not meet with you. When we face resistance and the buyer is hesitant to commit the time to meet with us, all of our energy should go toward selling the value of the meeting for the prospect. Our goal is to make it as easy as possible for them to say yes, and the way we accomplish that is to communicate the ROI (return on investment) to the buyer for allocating the time to meet. I even go as far as promising the prospect that they will leave our meeting with value and ideas even if there is no next step for me.

The Universal Objection Buster and The Money Line

Most sellers will only face a handful of typical objections: They're happy. They're under contract. There's no money. It's not a priority right now. They're busy. They're not looking for something. And occasionally, we will run into objections based on preconceived biases about our company, our product, or service.

Should we have concise, elegant, effective, articulate, prepared responses to these typical objections? Absolutely. There is no excuse not to. If you know an objection is coming, have your objection buster loaded and ready to fire back. Why should we feel the pressure of having to think on our feet when we can have powerful responses prepared?

As smart as it would be to have well-thought-out canned responses to common objections, I believe that when prospecting, there is a universal objection-buster that can do you more good than you'd ever imagine. I cannot begin to count how many times I have successfully deployed this response to any number of reasons prospects give for rejecting the initial request for a meeting. What is this ubersimple, universally applicable objection buster?

"Visit with me anyway."

These four words have proven to be so effective at convincing buyers to accept the second or third ask for the meeting (during the very same call) that I have come to call this phrase "The Money Line."

Regardless of the reason the prospect gives for rejecting a meeting request, simply acknowledge it, bounce off of it, and then tell the buyer to visit with you anyway.

"Joe, I understand you are under contract through next June. That's great. Let me ask you to visit with me anyway."

"Mary, it makes complete sense to me that you are swamped. I work with production managers (or whatever her position is) every day and totally get it. I am going to ask you to visit with me anyway. You are going get value and ideas from the meeting, even if there is not a next step for me."

"Awesome to hear that you are happy, Steve. Many of our clients told me they were happy when we first met, but today they're our biggest fans. Even though you are all set, visit with me anyway. I was hoping for an hour, but just give me 20 minutes to share a couple of the massive outcomes we are creating for DEF companies."

"Shari, I hear you that this is not on your radar right now. Actually, we hear that a lot because of the nature of JKL issues. The reason I'm asking you to meet with me, from what I can see, is that your company looks so much like several of our best clients who were not looking for a new solution when we first spoke, but we showed them opportunities to radically improve PQR performance. Even though this is not a priority today, visit with me anyway. You'll walk away from our meeting with several valuable insights, even if it isn't the right time to move forward and you will be much better positioned for when your company does decide to look at this."

I regularly receive notes from salespeople thanking for me for sharing The Money Line during a workshop. The notes almost always say the same thing. The salesperson is shocked how easy and natural it is to use "visit with me anyway" and they cannot believe how many meetings they are setting by simply being willing to ask a second and third time for the meeting using that line. Try it. You'll like it!

Instead of Dreading Getting Voicemail, Look Forward to It

We are told there are two certainties in life—death and taxes. And if you expect to create new sales opportunities via prospecting, you can go ahead and add a third. Voicemail.

People who preach that the phone is no longer an effective means of creating sales opportunities like to make voicemail into the bogeyman! They tell us that no one answers calls anymore and all calls end up in voicemail. Further, salespeople that don't want to or don't know how to prospect love to whine and complain that they're always getting voicemail.

Guess what? Most people don't answer their phone. Many hide behind voicemail. I have no argument to contradict that reality. However, not all calls go to voicemail, and even more important, voicemail is not a dead end. A proactive call that ends up in the prospect's voicemail box is not a waste. *Au contraire!* Voicemail is a gift to the salesperson, and my goal here is to help you see it that way.

Think about it. Voicemail is beautiful. You are not interrupting anyone. No one is trying to get off the phone with you. There are no rebuttals or objections coming back your way when leaving voicemail.

Instead of dreading voicemail, what would happen if you did what other top prospectors do? What might happen if you embraced voicemail, and instead of complaining about it, you actually looked forward to it? What if you had a positive view about voicemail and saw it as an opportunity to leave a powerful, thirty-second radio commercial for your prospect?

Time and time again, I have proven that you absolutely can be building a relationship with someone who has yet to call you back. When you get really good at leaving voicemails, you believe with certainty that some percentage of your target prospects are not only getting your messages, but also are getting value from them. Some are even enjoying your messages and looking forward to what you may do next.

How do I know this? Simple. Prospects have told me that they appreciated my efforts to reach them. Some commented on the variety of messages I would leave them. Others praise the creativity or humor. And as crazy as this may sound, many have actually thanked me for being persistent and not giving up. Sales friends, that is the experience I want you to have when you prospect. How incredible would it be if prospects were thanking you for "pestering" them? How much more confident and willing to proactively call prospects would you be if that was the kind of feedback you received? As someone who has done a ton of personal prospecting myself, and someone who has helped thousands of salespeople improve their proactive calling, I promise that you can up your own prospecting game too.

Get Creative. Be Unique.
Lose the Sales Voice and Hackneyed Phrases.

To win with voicemail our messages need to stand out. That means we must come across much differently than the typical salesperson who often sounds either like a robocaller just going through the motions, or a cheesy, inauthentic pitchman. No one is returning a call from a bored-sounding seller who, forgive the pun, is just phoning it in. And most buyers will hit delete the moment they sense a cheesy pitch!

There is no rule that your voicemail messages need to sound like everyone else's. In fact, I'd suggest the opposite. Format your voicemails so they are unique and intriguing. Be creative with how you share those customer issues/outcomes/talking points from your sales story. Focus the message around what's in it for the prospect. As quickly as possible, get past the introductory portion of your message and get into the meat of why this prospect should be clamoring to meet with you. Deploy the Bridge Line then pivot right into value nuggets that will get the prospect's attention. "Jeff, it's Mike Weinberg, The New Sales Coach. I'm helping CEOs who are frustrated with Issue A, struggling to achieve Result B, and excited to experience Outcome C . . ."

Take note of how quickly I moved into my powerful talking points. More importantly, take note of what I didn't say. Buzzwords. Hackneyed, overused phrases. Corporate speak. I want to scream (and injure someone) every time I hear a salesperson start a proactive call or voicemail messages with either of these way-too-popular phrases:

"I'm reaching out . . ."
"I just wanted to touch base . . ."

Do yourself and me a favor. Lose those phrases. Get counseling if you need to, but stop using both of those awful expressions now. Go cold turkey. Just stop. Trust me that they are not helping you because they are meaningless, overused, and make you sound like every other pathetic salesperson on the phone. There may not be a more common business expression this decade than "I'm reaching out." I cringe every time I hear that phrase. Nobody feels special or wanted because you are reaching out to them, and I can promise you that they definitely don't want you touching their base either! Frankly, that's icky.

Mix up your messages. I see so many sellers who keep leaving the same message over and over and then express disappointment that they are not getting called back. Similar to how buyers rarely accept your first attempt at requesting a meeting, most don't even think about returning a first voicemail from a sales-person. Think about how you respond to a message from a sales-person you don't know. Do you pick up the phone to immediately return the call, or like I do, say to yourself, "If it's important or this person is really serious about getting in touch with me, he'll call back." So if we know going into proactive calling that it will take multiple messages to earn a call back, then shouldn't we have a plan to leave a series of messages, each with its own twist?

Earn the Callback with Perseverance

When leading workshop sessions on proactive calling, this is my least popular piece of advice. No one likes hearing it, but it's the #SalesTruth. We earn the return call by persevering. More often than not, it's the persistence we show from leaving multiple mes-sages that convinces the buyer that we are worth a return call. I would love to tell you that it's your great voice tone, or compel-ling messaging, but most prospects tell me that it was the commit-ment being demonstrated that persuaded them to finally call back.

One of the big mistakes new proactive callers make is leaving too much time between messages to the prospect. Fearful of be-ing perceived as a pest, they'll let two or three months pass before leaving a second message and that kills their effectiveness. I re-peat: We earn the callback by persevering. A very big part of the reason prospects finally return our message is because we've left enough of them over a relatively short, finite period that they feel a sense of obligation to respond to our efforts. Said differently, we earn points by leaving a series of interesting, value-creating messages, and the cumulative effect from those messages is what compels the prospect to reciprocate. Whatever their emotion and thought process, be it professional courtesy, guilt, obligation, legitimate intrigue, or even a desire to just ask you to stop calling, it's the volume of quality messages received in a relatively short time-frame that catalyzes the return call.

Earlier this year an anti-prospecting salesperson at a company where I was conducting training publicly shared his frustration with voicemail in the hopes of persuading his teammates and me that proactive calling was fruitless because such a high percentage of calls went to voicemail. After his long and colorful rant decrying prospecting as a giant waste of time, he offered his closing argument. "I left eighty voicemail messages and did not receive one return call. This does not work!"

I began to smile as members of the sales team looked directly at me for a response. I am sure a few had their fingers crossed wishing I'd stumble in the hopes that their manager would let them off the hook for prospecting, but the majority were likely praying that I'd come up with a genius retort to put this negative, loud underperformer in his place. I smiled at Mr. Negative long enough to create discomfort and then asked a question. "Tell me this, Nathan, did you leave eighty different people one message each? Or, as we agreed during our training, did you leave twenty strategically selected target prospects a series of four quality messages each over the course of three weeks?" Nathan sheepishly confessed to only leaving one voicemail per prospect and everyone in the room knew it was doubtful he made more than a dozen outbound calls anyway.

Recently, during a group online meeting, a subscriber to my video coaching series asked me to expand on what I meant by my declaration in a video module that you can be building a relationship with someone who has not yet responded to your calls and emails. Before I could even answer, my friend Dominic Testo, from Upstate New York, jumped in. Dominic is a top-drawer sales hunter selling for a small company in the plastics business. Through his personal prospecting efforts, he has acquired more new major customers than I could name. We speak a few times per year, and it's been fun watching his sales star rise. I'm pretty convinced we'll be reading his bestselling sales book within the next few years. He's that good.

Dominic shared that one of his favorite things that happens after diligently pursuing a prospect is that when he finally gets the call back the prospect begins the conversation by apologizing. I have experienced this countless times myself, and I'm pretty sure most people who have mastered proactively pursuing target prospects have too. It's the craziest yet most beautiful thing. Someone who doesn't know us, someone who we've been "pestering" with messages via every means available (snail mail, LinkedIn, email, voicemail, referral introductions, etc.), someone who is incredibly busy, who knows we are a salesperson and owes us absolutely nothing, picks up the phone, calls us, and starts the conversation by saying, "Hi, Dominic, it's Susan Spanos with PQR Company. I am so sorry it's taken me this long to respond. It's been so crazy here and I really appreciate your persistence in trying to get ahold of me."

As many times as that has happened to me and as many times as I've heard salespeople sharing their exact same experience, I am still floored each time. It truly is the best reminder that not only does prospecting work, but that we are indeed in the process of building relationships with some percentage of the prospects we are pursuing—even though we do not know it. Yet. Be encouraged by this and use it as a motivator to invest the effort to upgrade your messages. Be creative. Work on your voice tone. Draft a series of relevant, compelling messages. Stop sounding like everyone else. For goodness' sake, lose the sales voice and the overused expressions. Commit to leaving multiple messages over a relatively short period. Personally, I like to leave messages about every four business days until I've left five or six messages. Then I take a break. But don't give up too early because experience shows that very often it's messages four and five that tip the scales causing the prospect to finally respond. Again, we are earning the callback with perseverance and creativity.

Befriend the Gatekeeper and Ask for Help

In the past, I didn't typically invest much energy in my writing and workshops coaching salespeople on dealing with gatekeepers. I wasn't intentionally avoiding the subject but (mistakenly) assuming it was something that came naturally to salespeople. There is also the reality that unless you are targeting very senior executives who actually have their own assistants serving as gatekeepers, or you do lots of in-person prospecting and come face-to-face with receptionists charged with keeping solicitors away, in today's environment we don't run into gatekeepers as often as in the past.

However, it turns out that there is a great deal of interest from prospectors who continually ask for guidance and best practices for dealing with gatekeepers. Many are intimidated or confused by having to deal with a live human intermediary.

My advice is simple. Treat the gatekeeper like a living emoting human being and be very intentional about doing just two things: Making a friend. Asking for help.

Yes, some people in gatekeeping roles can be snarky and difficult. Some have condescending attitudes and seem to enjoy disrespecting us. Others see it as their personal mission to protect the person we are trying to see, and they work to derail our every attempt to connect with the target contact. Even when all those are true, my best counsel is to befriend the gatekeeper. In all of my experience observing salespeople, I have yet to see a salesperson succeed in attempting to intimidate or power-over a gatekeeper. In fact, I have only seen disastrous outcomes from threatening or belittling the person tasked with protecting your contact from you. Typically, the harder we push gatekeepers the firmer they stand their ground, and creating an antagonistic relationship right from the outset generally isn't a recipe for success when it comes to developing new business. So, instead of positioning yourself against the person between you and your prospect, take a different tact.

Use your relational ability, your EQ, and your sales skills to create a dialogue with the gatekeeper. Pretend that this person is your prospect, and truthfully, for the time being, he is. Be kind. Be respectful. Be prepared. Be concise. Demonstrate that you understand their role and that you respect their position and their time. Don't make the mistake of assuming that this gatekeeper is unfamiliar with the business issues facing your prospect. Go ahead and adapt your messaging a bit, but you should absolutely feel free to share key customer issues and outcomes/talking points from your story. Let the gatekeeper know the why behind your motivation to get on the prospect's calendar. Make it clear that you are helping people (in similar positions) like the target contact and that she would receive value from investing the time to meet with you.

While you are scoring relational points by showing deference to the gatekeeper, take it a step further and ask for guidance and help. Most people like to help others who are in need, especially when they are asked nicely. So ask nicely! If I'm speaking with Steven who's an administrative assistant to Charles and charged with protecting Charles and his calendar, I will ask Steven to guide me.

"Steven, may I ask you to help me, please. What would you suggest is the best way to earn thirty minutes on Charles' schedule?" Or I might inquire as to what advice Steven has for someone looking to secure a meeting with Charles. The key here is to respect the gatekeeper and make him feel secure and important, yet at the same time, not just roll over and allow the person to shoo you away. It is up to us to convince the gatekeeper that it is in his and his boss's best interests to help get you in front of the boss. The more and better you are able to do that, the more meetings you will secure through gatekeepers.

Now that we've worked through what it takes to *create* new opportunities, let's transition to a few important best practices for advancing these opportunities through your pipeline.

RECOMMENDED RESOURCES ON PROSPECTING

Combo Prospecting by Tony Hughes

Eat Their Lunch by Anthony Iannarino

Fanatical Prospecting by Jeb Blount

High-Profit Prospecting by Mark Hunter

New Sales. Simplified. by Mike Weinberg

Smart Calling by Art Sobczak

CHAPTER 12

Stop Rushing to Present and Demo

Presenting is not the same thing as selling! It's usually only one small part of the entire sales process, yet so many sellers rush to present or demo their solution and blow right by the discovery phase. This hurts their effectiveness at advancing sales opportunities and diminishes how they are perceived by buyers.

In recent years this disturbing trend has only worsened. It appears as if much of the sales profession has forgotten the old adage that "discovery precedes presentation." Always!

There are two significant factors contributing to this degrading of good sales process. The first stems from a topic we touched earlier. Salespeople are living in reactive mode believing the myth that buyers proceed two-thirds through their process before engaging with sellers and therefore wait for prospective customers to approach them. This results in encountering buyers who are way down the path gathering information and examining options. These leads (prospects), while potentially highly qualified, are typically less amenable to allowing the salesperson to follow their own (good) sales process. Because these customers are already shopping and evaluating potential vendors before meeting with a salesperson, they feel more empowered to dictate the process. Since they are coming to us, they sense the freedom to request a demo (or a presentation) almost immediately, and compliant salespeople who don't own their sales process or understand the importance of doing effective discovery before presenting are all too willing to comply.

While many of today's experts counsel sellers to adapt their selling process to the customer's buying process, I take a contrarian perspective. Just because a prospect requests (or insists) on a demo or dog-and-pony show, that does not mean it is beneficial to your cause to provide one. In fact, I would argue that in most cases, it hurts your position and chances of winning the sale.

The second factor nudging sellers to present and demo prematurely is the proliferation of online meeting technology. It has become the norm, particularly in the tech space, to conduct early-stage meetings online and buyers assume that since they agreed to meet with a salesperson using a platform conducive to delivering demos and presentations—that is what they expect to get . . . demos and presentations. Weak, ill-advised salespeople, who either don't know better or haven't been coached how to overcome this expectation, follow the prospect's lead and execute premature presentations. While the marketing and product development people may love to add a tally to the demo count, the reality is that this premature presenting of solutions significantly damages how the salesperson and the company are viewed by the prospect.

Would You Trust a Doctor Who Wrote a Prescription Before Examining You?

Imagine this scenario. You don't feel well and make an appointment to see the doctor. It could be a brand-new doctor with whom you've never visited, or it could be your personal physician who you've seen for years. You wait for what feels like an eternity in the examining room while sitting uncomfortably on the table with that crinkly paper. While waiting, you become anxious wondering how the doctor will diagnose what is wrong with you.

The physician eventually shows up, apologizes for the long wait and then begins a long recitation about her background, specialties, and the current medical studies she's following. She then pivots to describing this wonderful new drug just released by one of her favorite pharmaceutical companies. The doctor waxes on and on about all the research and development that went into creating this new drug and then highlights the many benefits it produces for patients. Having not even bothered to examine you or inquire why you were there, she finally ceases the presentation, pulls out her pad, and writes a prescription for this must-have new medication telling you that she's confident this will hit the spot and be perfect for you.

Seems silly, doesn't it? Hard to fathom? You wouldn't think too highly of or have much respect for this so-called physician, would you? I would be running out that door as fast as I could and there's no way in hell I'd be filling that prescription. That doctor is a self-absorbed quack with zero interest in her patient's well-being. What kind of doctor writes a prescription prior to examining and diagnosing the patient? You can't possibly trust someone who operates that way. I'd even wonder if she had her patients' best interests at heart or whether she was on the take from the pharmaceutical company.

But let me ask, is this not the way many salespeople approach customers? Isn't that exactly what we do when we blow by the discovery phase of the sales process and start demoing our software or pitching our programs prior to thoroughly seeking to understand the customer's situation (current state, needs, threats, initiatives, challenges, objectives, and desired future state)?

It Is Impossible to Be a Trusted Advisor When You Pitch Before You Probe

Friends, I don't give a rip that in many industries it has become the norm that buyers expect salespeople to show up and perform like a trained circus animal. Those expectations are stupid and put the seller in a disadvantageous position. Similar to our reaction to the doctor pushing her favorite new medicine on us, how in the world can we expect the prospect to view us as a consultant, a trusted advisor, and an outside expert who has their best interests at heart, when we show up in pitch mode? When we start showing off our product prior to making even a half-assed attempt at doing discovery work, we immediately get downgraded in the customer's mind to vendor and pitchman status. Even when it is the customer dictating the process and asking us to present (prematurely), we still get perceived as nothing more than a vendor pitching our wares.

Nowhere is it written that complying with the customer's request or process guarantees us an advantage. In fact, I'd argue that often the #SalesTruth is that strictly following the customer's direction hurts instead of helps our position. Acting like a spineless lemming who doesn't "own" your own sales process, may score you "obedience points," but does not demonstrate in any way that you are positioned to deliver the most value or produce the best outcome for your prospect. Allowing the customer to dictate your process also prevents you from setting yourself and your company apart from the competition. Said differently, when we (and our competitors), in fear, do exactly what the customer asks us to do, we lose a significant opportunity to differentiate our approach and demonstrate our commitment to creating the absolute best possible solution for the customer.

Simple Reasons Most Presentations and Demos Are Awful

Aside from almost always being premature, there are other very simple reasons that presentations, webinars, and demos fall flat.

My biggest frustration with presentations is that the focus is wrong. It often feels like 90 percent of the content is about the company doing the selling, its merits, and its offerings. Instead of making the customer and its issues and desired outcomes the focus, sellers drone on with self-focused, uncompelling garbage. Of course, when you don't bother to do professional discovery work prior to presenting, it's pretty difficult to make the focus of your presentation what you discovered about the prospect and how you are going to address their issues and produce their desired outcomes!

Presentations, particularly online meetings and demos, generally move too slowly. The audience gets bored. Self-focused + Slow = Boredom. That's not a formula for sales success.

Lack of visual stimulation further contributes to boring presentations. A common critique is that most presentations contain too many slides. No one likes to make fun of irrelevant slides more than I do, but for online meetings, I actually believe sellers would do better by using more slides and quickening the pace they move through them. One of my biggest complaints sitting through my client sales team's online meetings and demos is they are not visually interesting. The slides tend to be dull, text-laden, and lacking in zeal. Lots of bullet points and very few intriguing images either induce sleep or tempt prospects to grab their phones and thumb scroll through email or social media posts rather than engage with the salesperson.

Everything I hate about bad presentations applies even more so to demos (online and in-person). My friend Kyle Ziercher coined a phrase after watching potential vendor after potential vendor demo software solutions at a company where we worked. He called it CCDH: Click, Click, Demo Hell. The salesperson, or tech person conducting the demo, just keeps on clicking all the while annoyingly announcing, "If you click here, ABC happens, and when you click here, we go to DEF, and clicking here shows us JKL." Click. Click. Demo Hell. The worst part of CCDH is that there is zero connection to the prospect's business issues. It's just a self-contained, self-focused, self-absorbed demo that might as well be conducted by a monkey or a robot because there is no evidence of any professional selling taking place. Selling requires pre-work and legitimate attempts to understand the customer's situation prior to presenting a solution.

What most tech salespeople do when demoing their sophisti-cated software platforms is no better than how the amateur sales-person behaved at the Audi dealership, when I recently walked in to look at a new car. I sat down in an A6 model parked in the showroom, and the salesperson jumped in the passenger seat next to me. Without asking a single question, he started demoing Audi's cool new multiscreen visual interface. For ten minutes, he went on and on and on about all the new features and function-ality. Ten minutes! He had no idea who I was, why I was there, what my objectives were, or whether I even cared about this interface. What this amateur did not know (because he didn't care to ask) was that I was interested in this car because I had read how quiet the A6's interior was while cruising on the highway and wanted to experience that for myself. But this "salesperson" was too busy executing his pre-packaged tech demo to learn what mattered most to his prospect. That was a costly demo misfire indeed. I walked out promising myself that individual will never get another minute of my time.

Observe and Critique Online Meetings and Demos from Afar

I was working with a SaaS company whose online demos were not resulting in as many scheduled next steps as the company's leadership expected. To get a better feel for what was taking place, I scheduled myself to observe a handful of upcoming demos conducted by various members of the sales team. For two of the meetings, I was present in the company's conference room where the salesperson and product expert were leading the demo, and I observed three of the demos remotely from my own office. The different experiences were striking. You only think you know how the meeting feels from the customer's perspective, but until you observe a few via the same means they do (remotely, online) you truly have no clue. Everything from that awkward silence and small talk while waiting for everyone to join at the beginning of the meeting to the distorted speakerphone audio quality hits you like a ton of bricks when observing demos remotely. Take this challenge: Commit to observing several of your sales team's demos and online meetings from a remote location. Watch and listen from the perspective of the customer. I promise that if you do this a few times that you will come up with significant improvements for how you conduct your own online meetings that will radically alter the experience for the prospect and your own effectiveness!

RECOMMENDED RESOURCES ON SALES PROCESS:

Baseline Selling by Dave Kurlan

Let's Get Real or Let's Not Play by Mahan Khalsa

The Lost Art of Closing by Anthony Iannarino

CHAPTER 13

Own Your Sales Process to Stay Out of the Procurement Pit

I posted a brief excerpt from the previous chapter on LinkedIn and created quite a stir. Sure, I was teasing the coming book launch, but more important, I was looking to remind readers that salespeople have rights, and that more often than not, blindly following the process dictated by your customer may not produce your desired result. For all the applause the post received from strong, successful, like-minded sellers sharing my perspective, it was interesting to see how many salespeople and buyers balked at my even suggesting that a salesperson could push back on the customer's procurement process.

Look, I get it. The role of procurement has expanded greatly in recent years. What we used to call "purchasing" got upgraded to "procurement." Larger organizations have larger and stronger procurement people, departments, and processes than we ever imagined could exist. These procurement professionals continue to grab and wield more power, often emboldened by their certifications and their mission. There's nothing more entertaining than seeing certified procurement and supply chain analysts with several sets of initials after their names (CPP, CSCP, CPSM, SCPro, SPSM) working to "level the playing field," neutralize salespeople, and commoditize their employers' purchasing decisions.

In response to my LinkedIn post, I was surprised to read so many sellers' comments defending their decision to, as a course of habit, default to their prospect's procurement process. Many went as far as declaring that we, as sellers, have no choice but to comply with the expressed wishes of the customer and that we'd be foolish and jeopardize our chances if we dared pushed back or suggested an alternative approach.

Before going any further, let me state for the very small minority of readers who do indeed sell to government organizations that, yes, I do understand that is a completely different situation and government regulations often legally preclude you from altering or avoiding your customers' processes. So for the one percent who are in that boat, by all means, follow the strict regulations within which you are forced to compete. But for the 99 percent of professional sellers not selling to governments, municipalities, and militaries, I offer these strong words of warning and exhortation.

Just because a customer asks for a demo or a sales pitch, does not mean that it benefits you to do so. And that is even more true when a customer instructs you to work through their procurement process or solicits a request for proposal (RFP). Most of us in sales are not paid to do work. We are paid to bring in new business and win deals. Said differently, there are no rewards for jumping through hoops, perfectly complying with some procurement weenie's ridiculous process, or for completing more pages of RFPs than other sellers. I'm sorry if this message offends you or upsets your apple cart, but I have some harsh news. Blindly going along with a buyer's direction simply for the sake of scoring "obedience points" is not going to help you bring in more business.

Too many salespeople wimp out on their own sales process and continue defaulting to the buyer's process even when it makes no sense. This deprives them of the opportunity to execute proper discovery work, enhance relationships with the right customer stakeholders, and prevents them from being able to tailor their approach, presentation, and proposed solution.

I understand that for many salespeople pushing back against the customer's suggested (dictated) process creates discomfort. We want to be liked. We want to be perceived as empathetic. We want to be helpful and responsive and respectful. We want to be easy to do business with. We want the prospect to want to work with us. Those are all great motivations and there is nothing wrong with our desire for a smooth relationship. But there's just one problem with what I call the "Acquiesce Approach," and it's a biggie. Acquiescing to the customer's strict process can prevent us from positioning ourselves as true advisers and consultants, stops us from differentiating our approach, and often ends up getting us commoditized as procurement lumps all potential suppliers together into the same box.

I can't speak for how much you enjoy getting stripped of the opportunity to differentiate yourself, your company, and solution, but I can speak for myself. I hate it! Getting commoditized sucks. Playing by someone else's rules whose desire is to squeeze all the creativity, differentiation, and profit margin out of our deals is not fun. Following orders from a certified procurement person whose stated mission is to "level the playing field" is not very motivating to me and certainly not why I am in sales.

I have two missions as a professional salesperson. First, I am driven to create the absolute best possible and highest-value outcome for the client. Second, I am committed to winning every deal for which I compete—assuming, of course, that I'm convinced that it is in the best interests of the client. Those two missions are what drive me and drive my sales process. I am beholden to getting the client what they need to win and doing what I need to do so I can win. The term "win-win" gets thrown around a lot, but this is one instance where it perfectly applies. I'm committed to creating a win-win situation and if that means having to circumvent, avoid, or alter the client's buying process, so be it. I don't work for procurement people. I work for my client contact (businessperson), for my company, and for myself. It's incumbent on me to do whatever is ethical and necessary to ensure the client gets the best solution and to give myself the best chance of winning. Translation: When I perceive that the customer's stated buying process or instructions to me are counter to either creating the best solution or improving my likelihood of winning, that's when it is time to stand my ground and push back.

Top Producers Are Usually Pretty Good at Telling Procurement to Pound Sand

Based on my experience from years of coaching salespeople at all levels of experience and success, I am confident that a good number of people reading this will not believe the following statement: Top-producing sales professionals regularly alter their customer's buying process. Regularly—as in doing so is the rule, not the exception. And if that #SalesTruth baffles you, let me take it a step further. Quite often, top-producing salespeople not only disregard procurement's directions and rules, they actually dictate to the customer how their companies will do business together. These top sellers change the rules, change the game, and change the outcome—all in their favor!

I so badly wish we were in the same room to have this discussion together. I'm smiling as I type this, picturing the very different reactions as readers process my bold claim. I can see the faces of true sales killers nodding their heads in approval and sporting smug smiles. I also sense the look of terror on other sellers as they shake their head, declare me clueless, and mutter "WTH is this guy talking about? No one gets away with that. There is no way I can push back against or change the way my customer buys." And there will be those in the middle of the spectrum, intrigued by the possibility of more boldly asserting themselves but fearful of the repercussions.

If you're already a believer, and like me, love both the feeling and rewards from telling procurement to "pound sand," enjoy the true success stories that follow, and I'll be right with you as you shout, "Amen!" To the cynics and skeptics, I may not be able to convince you that you have rights and that you might actually win more business by holding your ground instead of acquiescing to the prospect's every request, but I am going to try. And to those who fall in between, I implore you to read these real-life examples of small companies not only sticking to their guns, but actually pushing back against giant companies and their processes, declaring their own rules of engagement, and winning bigger, more profitable deals as a result.

These stories are very specific examples about three small companies successfully telling their giant customers' procurement departments and processes, "Thanks, but no thanks." Each of these companies have the belief, the guts, and the confidence that they bring so much value to the customer, and work so hard to establish relationships with the right key businesspeople within that customer that they have absolutely no trouble telling their contacts that they will not follow the procurement process because it benefits neither party. Said another way, the uberconfident people selling for these small companies have become very good at telling the procurement people to "pound sand."

These three companies have practically nothing in common. One is a small sales improvement firm providing sales consulting, speaking, and training services to an eclectic group of companies in a myriad of industries around the world. The second is a small company that provides services in the legal, HR, health insurance space to very large U.S employers, and the third company is a small-to-midsize specialty manufacturing company in the plastics arena. These three companies could not be more different except for the one common theme that the sales executives for each have decided, for their own reasons, that they will be more successful sticking to their sales process versus having process dictated by procurement.

Company One—Pound Sand Success Story

I'm intimately familiar with the smallest of these companies because it's mine! I'm the principal, and on what seems like a daily basis, I'm forced to decide whether I will follow my own sales process or that of a prospect. More than most sellers, I feel extra pressure to stand my ground and demonstrate solid process because I'm keenly aware that executives considering engaging me to help their sales teams are likely evaluating how I sell my own services.

Think about it. You're an executive looking to bring in someone to help your own salespeople become more effective at selling. Wouldn't you want to be assured that the person you are engaging for sales help can sell value and doesn't just roll over when the prospect attempts to dictate process or reduce the purchase to a commodity sale? That reality only strengthens my resolve when I'm asked about discounting my fee. It's actually fun to turn the table on my prospect executives and ask how they respond when their own salespeople come begging on behalf of

OWN YOUR SALES PROCESS

a customer for a discount or for silly payment terms. "Mr. Sales Executive Prospect, when one of your sales reps brings you a deal where their prospect wants your best product but is requesting a steep discount and extended payment terms, how do you respond?" That usually wins the executive over and they appreciate the conflict of interest and the paradox created by asking a sales trainer to give them a deal. However, on the rare occasion when that lighthearted resistance isn't enough and the prospect executive continues to push me even harder about reducing my fee, then I take the gloves off and punch back hard: "Let me get this straight. You want to hire me to stand up in front of your sales team and help them sell on value and avoid getting commoditized, but you are asking me to discount my fee? How in the world, with any integrity, can I teach your people how to own their own process and sell value if I do what you are asking and allow you to commoditize me? When you are introducing me to your people to kick off the session, are you going to read my bio and then brag that you got a deal? 'Mike Weinberg is a world-renowned sales expert and bestselling author, but we picked him because he caved and gave us a tremendous discount on his fee. Now pay attention as he shares how to win more New Sales and not allow prospects to treat you like a vendor and commodity seller!'" For the record, that response has worked Every. Single. Time. I've deployed it. And to my colleagues in the sales improvement business who "borrow" this approach, good for you. I'm happy to see you getting your full fee, too, and if you're not able to sell your own services without discounting, maybe it's time to look in the mirror and ask yourself some hard questions.

Several times per week my firm receives inbound inquiries, typically from midlevel people (nondecision makers) asking the same two questions. Their email or contact form submission goes something like this:

We are fans of Mike's content and very interested in bringing him in to speak at the XYZ Company National Sales Meeting. What is his availability and what is the price for a half-day/full-day/two-day session?

Before I share my team's standard response, let me ask how you would handle this type of inquiry from a hot lead? I'm especially curious about the reaction of those who balked earlier in the chapter, thinking I was crazy or clueless for even suggesting that we not immediately obey a potential customer's request.

I encounter salespeople every day who cling to the myth that being responsive, likable, agreeable, and easy to do business with is what wins you deals. Again, don't read what I'm not writing. There is nothing wrong with desiring to demonstrate all of those positive attributes. We should strive to be all of those and more, but the #SalesTruth is that being agreeable and obedient doesn't necessarily translate to value creation or justification of your premium price! Ignoring that argument, many sellers would still make a strong case that the only appropriate response to that unsolicited email inquiry is to quickly and fully answer the prospect's questions. They would tell me that the best, smartest thing I should do as quickly as possible is to reply with my available dates and pricing. After all, it's a hot prospect who's very interested and giving them exactly what they request as fast as we can will only make them want to do business with me even more.

As you have already surmised, we take a very different approach. Sales trainers are a dime a dozen, and I have zero interest in playing the commodity game where some nondecision maker researching options for a sales meeting or conference solicits available dates and pricing from who knows how many potential speakers. To me, this feels like a pricing exercise that will not result in the best solution for the prospect. Plus, I'm absolutely convinced that if my team or I respond to that request as submitted, we are actually hurting our chances.

Why is that? Well, first, how do I even know if I'm the right fit or best option for that prospect? And if I respond with dates and fees prior to doing any discovery work or gaining any knowledge of the prospect's objectives for this meeting, doesn't that telegraph to whomever the true decision maker (and business outcome "owner") is that I don't care about them? Not bothering to attempt to understand why they even initiated contact with me or what they are trying to achieve with their training/speaking event, screams that I'm not interested in truly helping them. I repeat again, it's very difficult to be perceived as a consultative seller who cares deeply about creating value for your client when you pitch and propose prior to doing proper discovery work!

Second, beyond what a lack of discovery effort communicates to the prospect, my next concern is more practical. I price my services at a premium—intentionally right near the very top of the market. There's a decent chance that my standard price for leading a workshop or delivering a talk won't be just 20 percent or 30 percent higher. Depending from whom else the prospect is seeking pricing, my fee could be two, three, maybe even four times higher. I cannot assume that prospect knows my reputation or the amount of demand for my services that justifies the fee structure. All I know is that they are soliciting bids and available dates and it's hard to imagine that I would win many deals in a price-driven process where there is zero opportunity to set myself and my services apart. I'm sure you feel exactly the same way about your business. You want every opportunity to learn what you can to determine if you're a good fit and so you can put yourself in the differentiated position where you have the best chance of winning. A premium price requires a premium sales process and offering up pricing and dates via email would not qualify as a premium process!

So instead of complying with the request, we push back and offer an alternative approach. Along with thanking the prospect for the inquiry, we immediately begin doing discovery work and ask a handful of questions in our response:

- We are curious who pointed you to Mike, which of his books have you read, and specifically, what is it about him or his approach that prompted your inquiry?
- What are your specific objectives for this meeting and what are you looking for this outside speaker/expert to accomplish?
- Along with yourself, which executives "own" the outcome of this meeting and will be involved in deciding who to use, and who else should Mike be speaking with during a discovery conversation to learn more?

Depending on the tone and specifics of the inquiry, we may also ask for more details about the event location, attendees, and whether dates are set in stone or flexible. This type of reply sends a clear message to the prospect that I'm serious about determining whether I'm a good fit even if that is not on their radar. It also makes it obvious that we are committed to a process and that while we appreciate being considered, we don't play fetch like a golden retriever simply because someone tossed a stick across the yard. This approach may also cause the prospect to wonder why other potential "suppliers" are not asking the same questions if they truly care about producing a great outcome for the client.

Even more than the message that type of response sends to the contact, how the prospect then responds to our attempted discovery speaks volumes to us and we can determine rather quickly if we are interested in proceeding or if it feels like a nonfit and potential waste of time. In case you are wondering, the overwhelming majority of the time, the contact is profusely thankful for our professionalism and desire to learn more, and in the very rare cases where our attempted discovery is rebuffed, that tells us all we need to confidently and respectfully decline the inquiry. What's amusing (and fun) is when that contact who didn't appreciate our questions and refused to engage in dialogue ends up having to come back later, reinitiate contact with us, apologizing and then acquiescing to our process because more senior people in their organization were either intrigued or frustrated that we backed away.

In this business it is even more important to stand our ground when we get down the path closer to a deal, not just early in the process. After suffering through my share of horrific experiences dealing with procurement people and their inane procedures (even after I had already struck a deal with the executives who decided to engage me), I made a major decision several years ago that has produced life- and business-enhancing results.

I reached my tolerance limit (and finally snapped) after yet one more procurement weenie sent over a master services agreement (MSA), along with the threat that in order to do business with their company, I must agree to the entire thirty-two-page document printed in eight-point legalese. Not only couldn't I understand most of the clauses, I was perplexed as to why there were so many sections in the document that seemed more appropriate for a contract software developer or a raw materials manufacturer. I also wondered why I should invest (waste) hours plowing through what felt like an irrelevant agreement in order to conduct a half-day sales workshop for a company that had already decided to use me.

In abject frustration and righteous anger, I tossed that mostly unintelligible thirty-two-page MSA in my recycle bin and called the procurement weenie who had just informed me via email that going forward, she owned the relationship with my firm and that she would be my main contact. As pleasantly as I could fake it, I told this twenty-six-year-old certified procurement analyst (with a very inflated view of her role) that I was tapping out. I had neither the energy nor the desire to spend any more time trying to decipher her nonsensical agreement and I was done. Then I said two more things. I let her know that she was not my contact at her company, the senior vice president of sales was. And then with a bit of attitude and glee, I asked the procurement woman to please inform the sales executive that I would not be executing the agreement and that I wished her well with the big meeting.

I immediately felt better even though I figured we'd end up losing that deal. Although I was sorry about hanging the SVP of sales out to dry because she was excited about the event we were putting together, the sheer relief getting to tell the procurement woman to pound sand more than made up for the money I was forgoing by walking away. It was quite empowering. More than that, it was an eye-opening lesson when later that afternoon the sales executive called apologizing for my terrible experience and their overbearing procurement processes. Then she asked if I would consider still doing their event if I didn't have to deal with procurement or sign their goofy MSA. At that very moment, I became a much better sales coach and consultant, and my life and my business changed.

Sure, in my almost twenty-five years in sales, I had run some pretty nice circles around procurement people and gotten pretty darn good at leveraging relationships with key business leaders and executives, but I had never gone as far as telling an over-empowered procurement person to take a hike, particularly at a company as large as this one. The senior vice president's apology call transformed my thinking and prompted me to do exactly what I did as a top-producing salesperson—attempt to replicate my success. As a sales hunter, when I tried a new technique and it worked, I would try it again. And again. And again. So, I figured that if telling procurement to pound sand worked at this company, I would try the same approach the next time I was faced with that situation. And it worked again. Finally, after a third triumph over the procurement process at a really large prospective client, I made an executive decision to adopt a formal new policy: Instead of dealing with procurement in a reactive manner, I would go on offense and proactively tackle the procurement people/process issue head-on!

What was this brilliant and formal new approach? I would inform the senior businessperson during our first discovery conversation that I don't do procurement, I don't do legal or master service agreements, and I don't bank my clients. With a giant smile, a positive attitude, and a large dose of confidence, I tell my contact that we decided a few years ago that 100 percent of my effort goes into creating value for clients and that I promised myself and my clients that all of our energy will be focused solely on creating and delivering the best speaking/workshop/coaching/ consulting engagement possible. Due to that commitment to my clients, I refuse to put even one ounce of energy jumping through procurement hoops, and regardless of what your standard (obscenely long) payment terms are, I get paid up front. That is our policy and it is not negotiable. If you can work with that, I'm excited to serve you, and if you cannot, I completely understand.

Along with the sheer pleasure from not being subjected to stupid, torturous, unfair, one-sided agreements, and not being treated like a subhuman vendor by procurement people and accounts payable clerks, there was another wonderful unintended consequence from adopting this policy. The senior executives and sales leaders at my clients absolutely love it! They applaud me for taking a stand against stupidity. They respect me for owning my process. They thank me for defending the honor of professional sellers and for proving that just because a prospect attempts to dictate the terms of a relationship does not mean you must comply. Even better, many client executives want me to help their salespeople adopt a similar approach, so they can create so much value for their customer businesspeople that they're able to resist defaulting to procurement's process too.

In just the past month, my team and I successfully deployed our dictate versus acquiesce approach three times. In the first scenario I was wrapping up an initial discovery call with a sales executive and his sales manager from the U.S. headquarters of an Asian electronics company. Trust me that you have heard of this company, and there's better than a 50 percent chance that you have their products in your home. It was pretty clear that the executive was intent on engaging me for a *Sales Management. Simplified.* Workshop, and before I could even bring up our policy, he stated, "I am excited to put this together with you and I will need to get our procurement team involved to firm everything up." I responded that I was honored to be selected to help increase sales management effectiveness in his division, but we might have a small issue. After explaining my decision to spend ZERO effort dealing with procurement people and processes so I could devote my full focus on creating and delivering high-value engagements for my clients, the executive responded with an audible, "hmmm" and paused. He didn't sound angry; he was more stunned. He said that he found my position "interesting" and that he would see what he could do on his end. There was no drama. No threatening me that if I didn't obey he would be forced to use someone else to help his sales managers. No begging or trying to explain how he really wanted to work with me but didn't see a path around his GIGANTIC company's policies.

Later that afternoon the sales manager called my assistant and gave her two different credit cards to put half of my fee on each. That. Same. Day.

The second scenario was a bizarre and pathetic attempt by an ineffective procurement analyst to put her fingerprints on a deal to justify her job. This situation was with a multibillion-dollar engineering and manufacturing company with US headquarters in New England and a European headquarters in the United Kingdom. I had done extensive work over a long period of time with another division of their company and had just come to an agreement with the senior vice president of this division to lead a two-day *New Sales. Simplified.* Workshop and provide access to my video coaching series to thirty individuals. We agreed on a fee that was lower than my standard fee for new clients. I was happy to offer this reduced rate due to the long-term relationship I had with his parent company through the other division.

The day after we finalized the engagement a previously unknown senior purchasing analyst contacted my assistant. Somewhat laughably she let us know that she would be handling the purchase order and was formally requesting that we offer additional discounts for both the workshop and video content. Mind you that this request came after the executive and I agreed to the scope and pricing of the engagement. I forwarded the purchasing analyst's email to my executive contact with this note:

Good morning, [SVP Name],

I teach salespeople to avoid people who behave like this. I'll respond with my regular price that is $10,000 higher per day and see if she prefers that.

Enjoy,
Mike

That is exactly how I responded to the purchasing analyst. The next day we received the purchase order for the amount the senior vice president and I agreed to. The. Next. Day. Purchasing defeated—again.

The third scenario involved a midlevel manager at a mid-size firm who was committed to engaging me to speak at their sales kickoff meeting and to provide *New Sales. Simplified.* video content to their national sales team. After speaking with me, and hearing very clearly that we don't bank our clients and full payment is due upon acceptance of the agreement, this manager then spent the next week emailing the two other members of my team, looking for a better deal and extended payment terms. At one point she even asked Shane, who heads up our content business, if we would accept half of the fee now and allow them to delay paying the balance for an entire calendar year, so they could spread the cost over two budget cycles. Shane's retort to her was perfect. He suggested that the manager go ask her president how he would handle a salesperson bringing that same request to him. Would he be happy to bank his customer by extending twelve-month payment terms? The next day the manager came back to us asking for instructions, so her company could wire us payment in full. We received payment The. Next. Day.

Am I sharing these stories about our success resisting procurement to brag? Absolutely not. But do I think there's a strong possibility as you read about my policy and how we have thrived from dictating process rather than acquiescing, you may not believe this is applicable to your situation? Yes, I do. My fear is that you will write off my examples as extreme—that you are telling yourself that I'm in a unique situation because I'm an author, or because I am my own brand, and while I can get away with such bold, unconventional sales behavior, there is no way you can pull that off and survive.

I could argue with you. I could tell you that there are dozens of sales authors and trainers with whom I sometimes compete for the same engagement and I am not in as a uniquely strong position as you perceive. I could tell you that there are plenty of hungry competitors who sell very similar offerings at less than half the price. In other words, I am not the only good option for sales improvement as there are plenty of lower-cost and certainly easier to work with choices. Most of my colleagues in the sales improvement space willingly jump through procurement hoops and accept the usurious payment terms dictated by large companies that somehow find it conscionable not to pay invoices from tiny little vendors for ninety days. So I could make the case that my situation is not as unique and different from yours as you might think.

However, I am not going to try to make any of those arguments. I will even concede that my position is a bit different because of what I sell and the fact that I'm the one who wrote my books. Because of what I do I may indeed be better positioned to leverage the desires of a senior executive against his or her own procurement people and processes. So, I understand if you're a skeptic and I won't ask you to adopt a dictate vs. acquiesce approach based solely on the personal successes I have shared. Instead, just mentally process my stories as "mind-openers" to get yourself thinking about the possibility of standing your ground and what that might mean for you. And now I want you to take a look at these other two small companies and the incredible success (and fun) they are having from deciding to change the rules and to stop playing their prospect's procurement game.

Company Two—Pound Sand Success Story

Company Two is a small firm comprised of only a few dozen associates. They provide a service around health insurance for very large US employers. Company Two sells to gigantic companies and their competitors, for the most part, are behemoths as well. You would recognize the name of every one of their clients and the majority of the companies they compete with that sell similar services.

It is common that companies going to market in search of new service providers engage consultants or brokers to help sift through options. These consultants often help design the request for proposal (RFP) that guides the selection process and typically work to keep potential new providers at arm's length from their client. The consultants believe they provide value by strictly controlling the search process. And if that's not challenging enough, once the potential new provider makes it through the RFP process, then it must navigate the behemoth prospect's legal and procurement departments!

Let me be clear. My client (Company Two) was very successful before I started working with them. Very. Their small firm was well known and well respected in the marketplace. Their blue-chip client list and track record of delivering industry-leading performance was beyond impressive. But senior management had grown tired of living as victims of large company strong-arm tactics and Company Two's win-rate on proposals was not as high as I believe it should have been based on their reputation, client success stories, and indisputable results.

We focused on a few areas to sharpen this firm's sales sword. We streamlined their bloated, self-focused messaging and drafted a laser-precise story around the major issues they addressed for large employers, the outcomes being achieved by their clients, and a handful of true differentiators that set their service apart from the competition.

We overhauled their process for conducting early-stage prospect meetings and prohibited them from presenting or even using a projector during first meetings with a potential client.

I convinced the CEO that part of the reason their proposal win-rate was not what it should be was because they were responding to blind RFPs without first having met with key stakeholders. He (reluctantly) agreed to adopt a policy that they would no longer submit RFP responses without first being granted access to key stakeholders for discovery meetings, which would allow them to better understand the prospect's situation and objectives for seeking a new provider.

The single most impactful change, however, was hiring the right sales hunter to spearhead the firm's sales attack. We clearly defined the role, articulated the required attributes and experience for the ideal candidate, and engaged a professional boutique search firm to lead the process. The stars aligned and after a yeoman's effort, the search team produced a candidate with whom I fell in love after one breakfast meeting.

Our new sales rock star generated a record number of meetings with ideal target prospects and beautifully implemented our sharpened sales process. The pipeline of new sales opportunities swelled and even though Company Two's typical sales cycle was six to eighteen months, our new hunter managed to close a few deals very quickly. Everything was going better than planned and then it happened.

Mr. Sales Rock Star, gaining confidence, began to proactively pursue our firm's dream prospects—the very largest companies in businesses similar to our best and biggest clients. He began initiating a relationship and seeking to secure a meeting with our number one dream prospect. After a few phone conversations and email exchanges, Rock Star uncovered that this prospect was considering going to market and evaluating potential new providers. Our excitement began to build until the prospect directed Rock Star to start working through their consultant. We obviously had mixed feelings about being redirected. The good news was that the prospect was serious about looking at options and the opportunity was heating up. The disappointing news was that it appeared as if we were going to lose direct contact with the prospect.

Sales Rock Star did a masterful job working the consultant, and while the consultant would not tip his hand, it was pretty clear that our firm would be fast-tracked to the group of finalists competing for the business. All along, Rock Star made it clear that we would not participate in an RFP unless granted access to the actual client for a discovery meeting, and the consultant understood our position.

Since this opportunity was so significant and this prospect would immediately become one of our largest clients, the CEO was keenly interested in our every move. And because he had been down this path before with similar sized companies, he began to warn Rock Star and me that we would have a hard time regaining access to stakeholders at the prospect.

As the days ticked by and the opportunity became more real, the CEO's intensity increased. I viewed my role as keeping him calm and helping Sales Rock Star stay on task. Honestly, I felt pretty good about the deal and based on what Rock Star was hearing from the consultant, it seemed like we were in a strong position.

The text messages from the CEO started coming more frequently. One evening he called me while driving home from work. "Weinberg, I'm nervous about this. My gut tells me that they are not going to grant us the discovery meeting prior to issuing the RFP, and once it's out, you know they are going to do that 'Cone of Silence' thing and tell us that it wouldn't be fair to take a meeting with us. What's the plan?"

I completely understood the CEO's angst, and I respected the fact that he had been down this road many times with other really large companies, but my counsel remained steadfast. "I hear you, CEO Name, but we need to maintain our position and continue to demonstrate confidence. Let the consultant worry about how we will respond if they deny us our requested discovery meeting. I'm convinced he has the power to get us in front of the key stakeholders at the prospect, and I want him feeling the pressure that we might actually walk away. How is he going to look to his client if the provider with the highest proven returns and strongest track record backs away—all because he strong-armed us? We aren't asking for anything crazy here; all we want is a meeting with the people who could be signing a multiyear deal with us. Let it play out. Sales Rock Star is doing a phenomenal job working every angle, and the consultant respects him."

A few days later Rock Star calls me after getting word from the consultant that we are indeed one of the finalist providers selected to receive the RFP. However, that good news also came with the heads-up from the consultant that it was not looking likely that we would get the opportunity to meet with the prospect prior to their letting of the RFP. I asked Rock Star how he wanted to handle it. He and I were completely aligned and decided to play hardball, at least for a little longer. Knowing that our CEO might get cold feet, we called him together. We patched the CEO into our call and provided the update. I'm smiling as I type this, remembering the enormity of the moment. This had the potential of becoming one the biggest deals in my client's history. We were all keyed up, and all of us wanted this victory so badly we could taste it. These are long-term deals, and huge companies like this don't go to market looking at new providers very often. If we blew this one, we might not see one like it for a very long time. There was a ton riding on this financially for both Rock Star and the CEO.

The CEO shared his heart. "Guys, I love you. I trust you, and I respect you, but you are killing me. You want us to tell the consultant controlling this process for the largest company in the industry that we are not going to submit a response to their RFP that we've been working to get for years—if they won't grant us a meeting? It feels very risky to me. Can't we win this thing on the merit of our response and our track record?"

Rock Star and I appreciated his concern and his question. We stood unified and stood our ground. I can't remember which of us said it to him, but we were in agreement. "To ensure a win, we need to get in front of the prospect. It's too big not to go for it. We have no idea what crazy nonsense the competition will throw into their proposals and we've lost deals in the past that we expected to win because we responded to RFPs without having developed any type of relationship with the actual client. Let's stick to our guns and let the consultant sweat a bit."

Rock Star went back to the consultant as graciously, kindly, and as firmly as possible informing him that we were honored to be selected as finalists but that we were reiterating our position that we will not be participating in the RFP process unless we are granted the opportunity to meet with the client's key players. The consultant was dumbfounded and asked Rock Star if he was sure about our position. Rock Star stood his ground. The consultant told him we'd hear back within twenty-four hours.

Early the next morning my phone rang. It was the CEO. "I don't know about this, Weinberg. What's the plan? Are we really going to walk away if the consultant comes back and tells us no? How are we going to respond because I'm pretty sure we are not getting this discovery meeting?"

The CEO exhaled a giant sigh of relief when I told him that we wanted to be assertive and sell from an abundance mentality, but we are not crazy! He almost kissed me through the phone when I said that of course we would cave and respond to the RFP if our request was denied. It's one thing to play hard ball but another to be stupid and cut off your nose to spite your face. At some point, after giving it your very best effort, it can make more sense to acquiesce than to walk away. We'd still have a one-in-three chance of winning the deal, even without gaining access to the prospect. But we had to take our best shot at doing this strategically, giving us the best chance of separating ourselves from the competition and winning the deal.

That afternoon Rock Star called. I could sense his euphoria before he even got the words out. "We got the meeting. In fact, it sounds like we are the only ones being granted access to the prospect's team." I'm emotional even now retelling this story because I had become friends with this CEO and I so badly wanted them to win this huge deal. It was personal to me. And while we hadn't yet officially been awarded the business, I knew this sales process victory gave us an exponentially higher likelihood of bringing the deal home.

The consultant and prospect stipulated two conditions for the meeting. First, we would only get thirty minutes, and second, we were not allowed to "pitch" the prospect. This was to be purely a discovery meeting. CEO, Rock Star, and I prepped feverishly to make the most of this thirty minutes, and I was thrilled not only to be invited to join them for the meeting, but that they asked me to kick it off.

After getting through rapport building I thanked the senior person from the prospect for honoring our request for this meeting. I shared that most of our client relationships lasted many years and that we had been serving some for more than a decade.

We wanted to meet with their team for two reasons: First, to ensure that our approach was a good fit for them culturally, and second, that we felt it important to hear directly why they were seeking a new provider and what they were looking to achieve by making a change. Along with thanking the senior executive for honoring our request, with a big smirk I shared that we would honor their request not to pitch or self-promote during our time together. Everyone from the prospect chuckled and whatever tension may have been in the room dissipated immediately.

We spent the next half-hour engaging in wonderful dialogue with the prospect. They were surprisingly transparent with us, and while we didn't technically "pitch" them, the way Rock Star and the CEO asked follow-up questions truly demonstrated our competence and the breadth of our expertise. As I was observing, the prospect team's voice tone and demeanor told me all I needed to hear. They were buying into my client's approach and personally enjoying Rock Star and the CEO. At the thirty-five-minute mark the consultant made it clear that the meeting was coming to a close. He turned to his client (the prospect) and asked if they had any final questions for us. The senior person spoke directly to our CEO and said, "This was very productive. Thank you for making the effort to meet with us. I like what we heard today, so let me ask, 'Do you feel like we are a good fit as a client for you?'" CEO started to answer, and I couldn't resist the opportunity to butt in: "CEO Name, stop right there. I'm afraid if you answer that question, we will be violating the promise we made not to pitch during this meeting." Everybody laughed. We exchanged pleasantries, and the meeting concluded.

The RFP was issued, we submitted our proposal, and were awarded the business! While it wasn't my sale and there was no financial reward in it for me, I still treasure that experience as one of the true highlights of my sales career. We stuck to our guns, executed our sales process, and instead of acquiescing to the giant prospect and their powerful consultant, we got them to acquiesce to us.

So, I ask the doubters and skeptics once more: Are you still convinced that you cannot push back against your prospective client's buying process? This tiny company successfully did so against their number one dream prospect and its high-powered consultant. Do you think that maybe, just maybe, you might increase your win-rate by asserting yourself and sticking to a process that puts you in a stronger position?

Company Three—Pound Sand Success Story

Company Three's success story is simpler and shorter. And what's fun about this one is that I was not involved in any way. This company become my client a year after this took place. I am simply relaying the story as conveyed by this midsize specialty plastics company's founder. I've heard him tell this story three times in exactly the same fashion, and I enjoy it every time I hear it.

One of the company's salespeople and the founder were working a massive customer. Well, stated more accurately, they were working with a massive company which, at the time, was only a relatively small customer of theirs. For confidentiality reasons, I cannot describe the customer in any more detail except to say that they manufacture a variety of name brand products and that you see their name on pretty much a daily basis.

Salesperson and Founder uncovered a significant production and quality issue being experienced by the customer and began working diligently to provide potential solutions. After testing several variations, they formulated a product that would meet the customer's needs and solve their issues. The new product was approved by the customer's engineering and production people and they turned it over to their supply chain management team (a more sophisticated sounding description for procurement weenies) to begin sourcing the new product.

All along, the Founder was clear with the customer's business-people (engineering and production) that he had no interest in working through their procurement process and he was "not going to fill out any RFP" (his exact words). Remember, the customer was a massive company with many billions in revenue and 100 times bigger than this midsize supplier.

Unbeknownst to the Founder, the customer's supply chain management drafted an RFP, obviously without his involvement. To say that the Founder was none-too-pleased when he received the RFP would be a severe understatement. He called his contacts at the customer. "What in the world is this? We do all this work to understand your problems and create a product for you and your purchasing people have the audacity to ask us to complete an RFP response? Are you kidding me? I told you that we don't work like that."

The Founder's contacts tried to assure him that they were on his side and that they wanted him to win the business. They coached him just to fill out the RFP and submit a proposal. The Founder was incredulous. "What do you mean you want me to win this? I told you all along what this product would cost, and I thought we had an understanding that if we created a product that worked, we had the business. I refuse to fill out your RFP. Period. If you want to work with us, you fill it out. We told you the price, and we did all this work to get you exactly what you needed. We are not responding to the RFP."

Days later the customer came back again, asking the Founder to please submit a response to the RFP. They made it clear they had no control over the process, and their hands were tied. He emphatically refused and repeated that if they really needed a response, they could fill it out for him and plug in the pricing they had already agreed to. Conversation over.

A week later his company received a huge purchase order for the product created for this customer, and years later they are still supplying that product.

Sales Friends, if the success stories from these three companies don't convince you that it is absolutely possible to own your sales process and push back against procurement when the prospect's process is not in your best interests, then I don't know what will. All three of these small companies are succeeding by imposing their process on giant customers, and they are winning bigger, more profitable deals and having loads more fun doing it!

· CHAPTER 14 ·

You Most Certainly Can Win with an Older Product or a Higher Price

When you spend as much time with salespeople as I do you hear a lot of whining. Salespeople are good at whining and finger pointing, and many become masters at projecting blame onto others for their lack of success. Why look in the mirror and accept responsibility for results when you can deflect and blame other things, people, and circumstances that are beyond your control?

For all the things that sellers love to bitch about—from unreasonable customers to cutthroat competitors, and from bad leads to a weak economy, two of the most popular, deadliest, and self-defeating complaints revolve around having neither competitive product nor competitive pricing. Said differently, weaker sellers often panic and become paralyzed when they don't have the best product and the best price. Ask any salesperson and they'll tell you with a straight face that sales would be much better if they represented a superior product (or service) or if what they were selling was priced lower ☺.

When You Live by the Product, You Die by the Product

News Flash: Your primary responsibility is not to educate potential customers about your company's products or services. Unless you are selling the latest, greatest, newest, coolest thing in a perpetually changing market, things tend to go poorly for sellers who make their product the star of the show or the focus of a sales call.

Think about the message the salesperson is sending to the customer when the focus of their interaction is the product. What does that communicate to the buyer? To me it screams that the salesperson doesn't give a rip about the customer, their situation, needs, challenges, or desired outcome. It says loud and clear that our relationship (using that word very loosely) is completely dependent on this thing we are selling. Further, it tells the customer, that you (the seller) and your company bring no value to this relationship. The product is forced to carry all the weight. Therefore, if you're fortunate enough to be the salesperson representing the latest and greatest product, you are destined for victory, but if you're the poor fool selling an older version or a supposedly inferior product, you're basically doomed and have no chance of winning. In fact, if that's true and you find yourself in the situation where you're up against competition with newer/better offerings, you might as well stop trying. Why even get out of bed or attempt to make living? You'd be better off putting effort into updating your résumé than trying to sell your dinosaur product.

I certainly hope you sense my facetious tone because as I reflect on my own sales career, I'm not sure I can even think of a time when I worked for a company with a demonstrably superior product. Now, I'm not saying we didn't offer better problem-solving, superior value, a superior experience, or even the best outcome for the client, but I am emphatically saying that in many cases, our actual product or service would not have won a beauty contest head-to-head against the competitors' offerings.

It's a complete and total myth that you must have the superior product to succeed in sales. If salespeople would put one-fifth the effort into sharpening their messaging and their sales skills that they do complaining that their company's product is outgunned by the competition, they would certainly win a lot more business!

I'm not declaring that it's easy to sell a crappy product or that we don't need to believe in the products and services we represent to customers. As discussed previously, to be truly successful in sales, it is imperative that we have the customer's best interests at heart and that we are motivated to provide a positive result that improves the customer's condition. If what we are selling cannot accomplish that, then there's an integrity issue and a real problem. But the vast majority of the time, that's simply not the case. The product we sell works just fine and is more than capable of meeting the customer's need, often better than the newer, cooler product does! Typically, the issue is that the salesperson is insecure about not having the absolute latest and greatest offering and is unwilling or unable to do what's necessary to overcome their product's deficit. Translation: They don't want to do the work necessary to outsell the competitor with the fresher offering.

The reality, however, is that product superiority and technology advantages are usually both temporary and fleeting. Competition in free markets is such that the breakneck pace at which new products are developed and released means that even if you are blessed to have the premier product, it's likely to remain that way for only a short season.

I've noticed that in just about every sales organization there are people who thrive selling their company's existing products and those who struggle selling the exact same products. One of the most dramatic examples of this played out in a company where I was conducting training at a time its leadership was pushing the sales force very hard to increase market share in a product category where they had the most dated product on the market. Dated is probably too gentle a description. These salespeople were selling a decade-old heavy equipment model against competitors who had released a brand-new model over the past two years. There was no hiding from the fact that my client's team was selling the same ole, same ole thing while their competition was out with sexy, shiny new toys brandishing all kinds of fresh technology. It wasn't even close to a fair fight, but the leadership at my client was very public and very adamant that they were committed to gaining market share in this category, two years prior to launching their own new model.

As I traveled the country it was fascinating to observe what basically amounted to the two distinct camps that had formed. There was a small minority of the sales force comprised mostly of high-performing reps that took management's mandate seriously. These reps understood and accepted the importance of the mission. For years they had been successfully selling this product and were not the slightest bit fazed by their competition's new heavy metal. Like many sellers, they loved a good fight and since they also loved their company, they prepared for battle as instructed by their leaders.

The second camp was filled with average and underperforming members of the sales team. The reps in this camp flat out refused to even attempt to take share from their competitors. These salespeople were not proud, didn't believe they could move the needle, and felt no shame in admitting an external locus of control. The reps in this group viewed themselves as victims of their circumstances and could not envision a way that their personal efforts might affect a different outcome. I'm not a psychologist, but this much I do know from exposure to a few hundred sales teams and thousands of sellers: When you don't believe you can sell something, you are correct. So instead of even making a half-hearted attempt, the reps in this camp simply punted. They didn't even try.

What was truly amazing is the incredible success the top producers from the first camp had taking business from their competitors. These people went out like true hunters whose family's food supply was dependent on them bringing home a deal. I wasn't shocked by the number and size of the victories secured by these driven hunters, but I sure was impressed. At the company's next major national sales meeting, several of the reps were brought on stage to share the stories of the major successes they had achieved "conquesting" new accounts in this product category. The company even went as far as sending film crews out to large customers who had placed big orders for this older model. They created powerful mini-documentaries interviewing these customers who shared their backstories and the why behind their decision to switch portions of their fleet to my client's equipment.

As a sales geek, I was moved. It was emotional as the lights came down in the big meeting room and the success stories/documentaries were played. There is nothing quite like hearing customers, in their own words, describe why they made a purchase decision, their excitement about how well that decision turned out, and the positive outcomes they're now experiencing. As each short video ended the audience erupted in applause and the salesperson who put the deal together went to the podium to share a bit about their approach to the customer and how they won the business. Sitting there listening, I could not help but wonder what the reps in the negative naysayers camp were thinking as their colleagues were being lauded for doing what these underperformers declared impossible.

There were four common themes I heard from those who, against the odds, went out with their ten-year-old model and took business from the competition:

1. **Fearless**. The reps on stage sharing their success stories knew no fear. To them, it was a game, and they were playing to win. They made it fun and recognized there was nothing to lose. These reps had a track record of success and believed if they put their best effort forward, they would indeed take share from their big bad competitors. There was no cowering in fear and no complaining about being outmatched by newer competitive product. They also relished the opportunity to prove themselves because they knew full well that their ancient product line could not win the feature-set beauty contest on a spreadsheet. These winning reps were fearless in finding unique ways to approach customers and set themselves apart.

2. **Focus**. The reps on stage sharing their success stories at the sales meeting all confessed to being laser-focused on the mission to increase market share in this category. It didn't happen by accident or luck. They heard the challenge from management, accepted it, and then refocused their calendars and their energy to execute the mission.

3. **Fit**. These winning reps were very strategic regarding whom they targeted for conquest business. Because they had a good sense of the type of customer who best resonated with their existing product, they went after accounts with similar profiles. In other words, they picked their shots and put significant effort into making those shots count.

4. **Familiarity.** Probably the most impressive thing I heard was how these successful sellers turned what most thought was a liability (their dated equipment model) into a competitive advantage. That's right. An advantage. These creative reps were able to craft a very different narrative that played off customers' challenges, frustrations, and fears with the newer models in the marketplace. The reality was that everything was not perfect with these new, high-tech, sophisticated models. All that glitters is not gold, and there were plenty of reliability issues with these new models. In many cases, customers were experiencing significant downtime, and operators were not as in love with all the new technology as they initially thought they'd be. From meeting with many customers using this new equipment, which by the way, is a best practice of top salespeople (getting in to see your competitor's customers instead of just overservicing your own favorite accounts), my client's top reps began to understand the critical angles they could work playing off these customer frustrations. These top reps flipped conventional wisdom on its head and successfully made the case that newer isn't always better, and in some mission-critical cases, it's actually dangerous. So instead of being intimidated to sell against the big, bad competitors' shiny new equipment, they looked forward to it! These successful sellers went right at the Achilles' heel of the newer models and convinced many fleet managers and executives that they were better off (for now) with familiar, proven, tried and true product that they could trust to get the job done. And if that argument wasn't enough, these top reps also went out and got testimonials from operators

who were more than happy to express their love for the traditional product from my client and their deep disappointment with the quirkiness and unreliability of the new models their company had purchased.

Friends, that is some real selling and exactly what prepared, driven, professional salespeople do. Just to finish the story, two years later my client finally did come out with its long overdue, brand-spanking-new model, and it is fabulous! Would you like to guess which "camp" of salespeople is having the most success (and most fun) selling the fancy new model? Correct. It is the exact same group that was most successful selling the old, outdated product. Imagine that. Maybe it isn't the product after all.

If You Need the Lowest Price to Sell, Then You Aren't Needed as a Salesperson

Please forgive me in advance as I administer some much-needed tough love to salespeople who repeatedly whine that their company's pricing is too high. If you get the sense that I'm scolding amateur sellers and yelling as you read this, then you are perceiving my tone correctly. When I teach this topic during live workshops my volume invariable increases and my face gets red. This one is personal because it's about the reputation of our profession and the role we play for our companies.

Even worse than throwing in the sales towel for having to sell an older or slightly inferior product are salespeople complaining that they can't make a sale because their offerings are priced too high! These sellers are the first ones to come back to management seeking discounts and declaring that "this customer is a price buyer." What I typically find, however, is that it's the insecure seller who is the one prematurely bringing up price with the customer in the first place. The scared, amateur, ill-equipped, and ill-prepared salesperson freaks out realizing that competitors have lower prices and is unsure what to do about it.

I do not know of a union representing professional salespeople, but if one existed, I'd run for a seat on the board and offer to be chairman or president. I'm indeed that proud to be a sales professional, and I so badly want the profession as a whole to raise its game. And if I ever was granted the opportunity to serve in a leadership capacity of an organization representing the best interests of professional salespeople, I would immediately make several declarations, of which this would be one of the first:

> **Members of The United Sales Professionals of America shall be strictly prohibited, under any circumstance, from complaining that their company's pricing is too high. So let it be written, so let it be done.**
>
> —Mike Weinberg, President,
> The United Sales Professionals Union

Why am I so adamant that we must never ever ever ever complain about our higher prices? There are two very easy, very simple, and very practical answers:

1. **Job Security.** It's the job of a professional salesperson to justify our premium price. Key word: JOB. That's what we do! Our job is to articulate and create value to justify the fact that what we sell is higher priced than what our competitors sell. It's truly that simple. Our higher priced products or services provide us job security. Think about it. If we had the lowest-priced crap in the market, our

companies would not need to employ us. They could simply post the price on the Internet and proclaim to the world, "We've got the lowest price crap right here. Come and get yours now." Seriously, who needs highly compensated salespeople to sell the lowest priced offering? Please stop complaining that your products are priced too high because that's akin to admitting that you are unable to do one of the primary jobs that justifies your existence.

2. **Compensation.** You know that nice base salary some of you have? Or that generous commission plan? Those expense reimbursements or the entertainment budget? Where do you think that money comes from? Darn right. The money that pays you comes from the gross margin we are able to capture when we sell something. Gross margin results from our ability to sell products and services above what they cost. Our companies pay us from that profit margin. Profit is a good thing, not a dirty word. So when you complain that you can't sell at the price your company wants to charge in the market, that's like telling your employer that you don't want to be paid at the same rate. Not sure how you feel about it, but to me, that's not the best move. And as president of our sales union, I would ask you to reconsider your approach.

Being priced above the market is a good thing. Higher prices communicate higher value to the customer. Frankly, I could make the argument that in many cases it would be more difficult articulating the value you create when your price is too low. Customers are not stupid. Everyone knows that there is no such thing as a free lunch, and buyers are rightfully suspicious when hearing that you have the best offering and the lowest price. That doesn't make sense and people understand that they get what they pay for. My dad has another great expression that my kids love to quote. Buy cheap, get cheap. It says it all.

Last year, Anthony Iannarino had one of his very high-end clients invite me to lead a few breakout sessions on prospecting at their annual sales kickoff. One of the treats for me was getting to listen to Anthony deliver the keynote talk to the sales team. He is a great speaker and I learn every time I hear him. His client sells fractional private jet ownership priced at the very top of the market—and for good reason. During his talk Anthony tackled the highest-price topic head-on. He chuckled telling the sales force that they were lucky their prices were so high because it gave them plenty to talk about with potential clients. Their pricing structure created the perfect opportunity to describe the many differentiators (including extra safety precautions and redundant crews and aircraft) that this company provided compared to its competitors. Anthony asked this team to consider how hard it would be selling for their lowest-priced competitor. He joked wondering what in the world those salespeople would talk about with prospects because their bargain basement price precluded them offering similar service levels to clients. And when you really think about it, how many super-high net worth individuals, the kind of people in the market for fractional jet ownership, are looking for a provider who cuts corners to offer a lower price? My gut tells me these clients would be more than happy to pay a premium, knowing that when they're flying (often 43,000 feet above the earth) on their own private airline that it is indeed profitable and positioned to provide the absolute highest standards when it comes to service and safety.

If you think that you can only succeed in sales with the very best product (or service) or when you have the lowest priced offering, I would question whether you truly understand the job of a professional salesperson.

CHAPTER 15

Two Extraordinary Sales Professionals' Not-So-Extraordinary Keys to Success

O ne of the biggest blessings doing what I do for a living is the opportunity to observe, learn from, and befriend some incredibly talented salespeople. I could not be more thankful for the relationships I've built and the lessons I've learned during the dozen years as a consultant and coach, and the dozen years prior to that working in sales.

When outlining my thoughts for this book, I felt compelled to include a chapter on the best practices of the very best sellers I've encountered. As I pondered how to present the information and struggled deciding which of the many truly great salespeople to highlight, the same two names kept coming to mind: Tom and Ron. What's interesting about these two men is that neither work at clients of mine. And even more intriguing, these two men are polar opposites. They could not be more different in their personalities, their styles, or in what they sell.

Tom is the top Volvo car salesperson in North America, happens to work at my local dealership, and is the only human being on this planet to have sold me more than one automobile. I am a car nut, have purchased twenty-six cars in my lifetime, and as you may have surmised, am also rather opinionated about sales. Tom is the very best there is. Bar none.

Ron has been a top producer in the corporate financial services industry for more than two decades. He is a dear, dear friend, trusted adviser, and a mentor. At pivotal moments in my life, he's one of my very first phone calls. He has cheered me on as my business and platform have grown, and he's the one who asks the most challenging questions.

Tom is fun, fashion forward, and relatively public. Ron is serious and conservative, dresses the part sporting his Allen Edmonds, and is more private. They are both as competitive as you can imagine, numbers and results driven, and as hungry as ever. Both have plenty of hardware in their offices demonstrating their consistent status as top producers. In fact, Tom is so important to Volvo that factory workers at the Gothenburg, Sweden, plant know him by name. And Ron has personal notes of appreciation from C-level execs at his gazillion dollar company. These guys love what they do, have a blast doing it, but are dead serious about playing to win and staying on top.

I sat down with each of them before crafting this chapter. I probably didn't need to interview Ron because we know each other so well, but I wanted to provide an opportunity for him to fill in some blanks for me. Because Tom moves so fast and most of my conversations with him are very brief, I managed to pin him down for a sushi lunch where he attempted to answer my questions between texts and calls from customers. His pace is beyond what I can process and his ability to multi-task exceeds that of anyone else I know. There was actually a day at the dealership when I watched him close a new sale, send a prospect out on a test drive, deliver a new vehicle, and handle a service issue, simultaneously—while smiling the whole time and making others smile as well.

Mind boggling.

These "formal" conversations with Ron and Tom only confirmed what I see day in and day out with my client sales teams. There is nothing magical about what the top salespeople in the world do. They work really hard. Really, really hard. They are really competitive. They go the extra mile whether they're prospecting, prepping, probing, presenting, proposing or following-up. They know their business and their competitors. And beyond their incredible work ethic and resolve to win, they understand that winning the sale requires connecting with the customer on a personal level. Before reading on, go back and reread this paragraph. So many people in sales are looking for the shortcut to success, but there are no shortcuts. Everyone wants the trick, the secret, the hack. But there are none. The best car sales guy and the best corporate B2B sales guy on planet Earth work their asses off—still! After years of being on top, they continue working their asses off and working to master the basics of selling. Please ponder that #SalesTruth. There. Are. No. Shortcuts. Hard Work + Mastery of the Basics = Top Sales Performer.

Tom is so good at what he does and seems to love it so much that I could not wait for the chance to sit down, outside the dealership, and just talk sales with him. The retail car business is a great mystery to most of us, even to car nuts like me who devour car magazines and websites. I was looking forward to getting more of the inside scoop and hearing the thoughts from the only person in my thirty years of car buying who earned my respect enough that I sought him out a second time.

No, when Tom was young he did not see himself in the car business and never envisioned achieving the level of success he has. He repeated several times that part of what keeps him sharp and focused is that the business is so hard and requires so much energy to stay on top. I pressed him from several angles on specifically what it is that sets him apart that has allowed him to personally sell exponentially more cars than the typical dealer salesperson. As hard as I tried to crack his code, all his answers pointed to the same basic theme: He goes above and beyond what his colleagues do. Sure, he admits that his DNA fits the business and his values and taste align well with the brand, but Tom sweats the details and leaves nothing to chance.

Just last Sunday I was standing in the kitchen with my wife after returning home from church. I was about to head to a café to write this very chapter when my iPhone rang. It was Tom, so I held up the phone to show Katie, who just shook her head. Bizarre timing.

"Tom, you can't be calling to tell me how gorgeous my family looks on the Christmas card because you won't receive it until tomorrow. To what do I owe the pleasure of this Sunday call?"

Tom responded that he couldn't wait to see the card, told me to give his best to Katie, and said he was calling because we just drove past each other on Manchester Road and he wanted to say hey. The reason we drove past each other is because the dealership is between church and my home. That's Tom—working on Sunday to line up the week ahead for maximum productivity. That's Tom, keeping in touch with his customers even when they're not shopping. That's Tom, being likable and enhancing relationships. Of course, I couldn't resist and had to ask how his year was finishing up. He said that it would be very close whether he hit his number. It would come down to the last few days and timing of deliveries. Keep in mind that Tom's number is probably five times the typical car salesperson's number, so it's all relative.

During our lunch meeting, I asked Tom how he set himself apart from others in the business, particularly in light of the negative view of car salespeople and lack of trust consumers have toward dealerships in general. Tom said he does everything possible to come across as the anti-stereotypical salesperson, and the key to accomplishing that objective is how the entire process feels to the customer. His primary goal is finding the right fit—the right car for the right customer. As Tom shared his sales philosophy, I delved further, hoping to get him to unpack his discovery process and how he learns what he needs to know about prospective customers. Interestingly, he does a lot of probing and discovery, but says that he often doesn't even realize he's doing it because it's his natural curiosity. He truly wants to know why they're there and what's important to them. Tom says that very early on in this dialogue with prospects he mentally puts himself in the customer's shoes and begins to imagine what the perfect car is based on what he's learning about this person's desires, values, needs, ego, and so on.

As someone who has gone through this process with him twice, all I can say is that he gave me a very different feeling than anyone else from whom I've tried to buy a car. It truly felt as if he were taking in all the variables that mattered to me, so he could present the perfect answer. It seemed much more like he was looking to create a bespoke, custom solution rather than put me in a car that happened to be available. As I pressed him to share more about his process, I got a glimpse of his obsession with preparation. Tom believes that if he does his job right and gets a good feel for what's important to the customer and his or her color/taste/visual preferences, there is a very good chance that the first car he shows will be the one the customer purchases. He's convinced that the first look the prospect gets of the car is critical, so he never rushes the process. In fact, he is so obsessed with making this first encounter perfect between the customer and the potential new car that he is fanatical about how cars on the lot are prepositioned.

I was in awe as he described the amount of work he does on a regular basis to know exactly where different models, different exterior/interior color combos, and different option-packaged cars are on the lot. But he doesn't just need to know where they are, he needs to be able to get to them fast without having to jockey a bunch of cars that may be in the way of the one he wants. The whole thing is a giant Jenga puzzle, and he refuses to have his process and his customer's first impression jeopardized by not being able to show them the exact car he believes is the perfect fit. Just for grins, contrast Tom's obsession with doing this well with the typical test drive experience at most dealerships. As a perpetual car shopper, can I tell you how many times a salesperson took forever to bring me a dirty car in a color combo I didn't like, that wasn't optioned the way I wanted and barely had enough gas to make it to the gas station around the corner?

What I most want you to take away from Tom's passion and work ethic is that this highly compensated, award-winning, top seller spends a whole lot of his off hours doing grunt work backstage that no one ever sees. That enormous backstage effort sets him up to succeed when he's frontstage face-to-face with customers. Please don't blow by this point. Tom isn't lucky, and he doesn't wing it hoping to guess right and present the right car to the customer. He prepares like a professional. And as fanatical as Tom is preparing for time in front of the customer, just wait till you read about Ron's process for preparing his teams to present in the boardrooms of his gigantic prospects. There is a consistent theme here that applies to every top producer I know. Preparation is not optional, and the most successful, professional salespeople invest the most time prepping and practicing for customer meetings and presentations.

The very first day I met Tom, I felt like he understood me. A new model was just released and while I had not previously fancied myself as a Volvo guy, there was just something about the unique look of this gorgeous car combined with the unique positioning of the brand. After having owned all of the marquee German luxury brands, I was ready for something different but wanted to be assured that the car I purchased sent the right messages to prospective and existing clients, who undoubtedly would form opinions based on the car I drove. From his probing, Tom sensed that this was important to me, and I could sense the light bulb in his sales brain turn on as he got an idea. He asked me to wait at his desk while he ran to grab the car he thought would be perfect. In what felt like less than a minute, he showed up in an immaculate new car dressed in ember black metallic over beechwood (baseball glove color) leather. It was drop-dead gorgeous. When I walked around to the driver's side to start the test drive, Tom didn't get out of the car. Instead, he lowered the window and said: "Not yet. Hop in the passenger seat." This was different, but I liked that he had a plan, and it made me feel like I was with a thoughtful pro.

We drove about a mile to a local park. I wasn't sure what he was up to but went along because he was so confident. He pulled over at a place where I could see the entire loop that cars took around the perimeter of the park. He kicked me out of the car and asked me to just watch as he circled the park and approached from various angles. For the next few minutes, I stood there as he drove *my car* around the park, so I could experience it the way my clients would as I pulled up to their offices or picked them up at the airport. When Tom finally came back, he explained his thinking and I realized that I was in the presence of a sales genius. He not only listened to me but wanted to ensure that this particular car addressed the number one concern I had shared with him. It certainly did. I drove the car for a few miles and headed back to the dealership to buy it. It was the most fun, professional, and painless car purchase I had ever experienced. And I'm 100 percent confident that I negotiated the price less intensely and paid more for the car because of how much I enjoyed Tom and his process.

I wish I could share more of Tom's secrets to success with you, but after knowing and watching him for seven years, and sitting down with him specifically to talk sales and best practices, I am even more convinced that he doesn't have many secrets. He loves what he does, and his heart is fully engaged in his work. He's indefatigable and as competitive as all get-out. He takes his business personally and takes full responsibility for his results. During our lunch, Tom casually asked me how my friend Donnie was doing. Tom had sold Donnie two cars but mentioned that he had not seen him in a while. I felt terrible having to tell Tom this, but looked him in the eye because I wanted his immediate reaction. "Tom, this is awkward, and I hate breaking the news to you, but Donnie actually bought a certified pre-owned Volvo from another dealer. I am sorry to break that to you." Tom pursed his lips and shook his head gently. Then the first thing out of his mouth was worth triple the cost of the sushi: "Ouch. I hate that, and that's on me. I should've done a better job keeping up with him."

I was floored by Tom's reaction. No one, and I mean no one, does a better job getting to know and keep up with customers than Tom. Tom knew Donnie, his family, his preferences, and so on. And Tom was constantly initiating contact. But take note of his reaction to hearing that he had lost (at least temporarily) a long-time customer. Did he blame the competitive dealer who made a low-ball offer to steal his customer? No. Did he accuse the customer of being irrational or cheap? Nope. Did he blame his own company for not supporting him well enough? Not at all. Where did Tom immediately place responsibility for losing a sale? Directly on himself. What a rare and refreshing reaction!

To help end our interview on a more positive note, I asked

him to share a fun recent sales success where he really had to fight for the win. He told me a story about a woman who had bought cars from him for years but whose husband was a loyal Mercedes guy. She got her husband to look at the largest Volvo SUV, but he seemed committed to purchasing yet another Benz. Tom gathered every bit of intelligence he could about the husband's preferences and picked out what he believed to be the perfect car for him. The next Sunday morning, Tom filled the gas tank of that beautiful new Volvo and parked it right in front of this couple's home. Tom texted the wife, letting her know that he left the key in a flower pot on their porch and hoped they would enjoy the car. On Monday, the couple came in together and purchased the car.

As we were leaving the restaurant, I thanked Tom for investing the time with me and then asked how he kept himself humble and hungry after having been on top for so long. As serious as I've ever seen him, he looked at me and stated as plain as day: "Mike, I never take this for granted. I stay humble because the business is so hard, and all of this success could go away tomorrow if I let myself get complacent."

As different as Tom's business and personality are from Ron's, I see the very same drive, focus, humility, and work ethic in Ron, maybe even more so. I've enjoyed a front-row seat as Ron's career has progressed from prospecting his way into small and midsize companies to his current position where he works on the very biggest deals with the very biggest companies. If my life depended on winning a long, complex, hairy sale to a giant company, without blinking I'd put Ron in charge. And truth be known, I'm pretty sure he and I would both agree that if push came to shove, he could outsell me. He's so stinking good, works so stinking smart, and so stinking hard. Even after having watched him crush it year after year, he still amazes me when he describes what he's working on and how he preps his teams for enormous customer meetings.

What I find most surprising is that while Ron is in what feels like such a sexy, appealing business—representing one of the best known and most respected financial management firms in the world and selling to the biggest and best US companies, most of what he does to win giant deals is very unsexy. Many of us in sales like to fantasize about what the very best salespeople do when selling the very biggest deals for and to the very biggest companies. Well, having watched Ron do this successfully for years, what I am about to share may disappoint you. While Ron is a special human being whom I love dearly, and he's smart and focused and mature and wise and disciplined and has just the right temperament to thrive in the industry in which he sells, the #SalesTruth as best as I can surmise is that Ron executes the fundamentals of large-company business-to-business selling better than anyone I've met. He is the very best in his entire industry because he is the very best at the basics.

If you were to poll Ron's coworkers, including everyone from the executive suite to the client service teams or to a person, each and every one would tell you that he is fanatical about these particular aspects of selling:

1. **Preparation.** Ron is the poster child when it comes to preparing for customer meetings and presentations. He leaves absolutely nothing to chance. As crazed as Tom was about setting up the cars on his lot to give him the best chance of presenting the perfect one, Ron is more crazed about learning everything he can about his prospective client's situation and then preparing his company's team to meet with that prospect. Everyone at his company understands that if it's Ron's deal, then they

are going to be asked to do more work on the front end. In fact, Ron shared that over the past few years, he actually invests more energy selling internally, getting team members ready to go face-to-face with prospects, than he does selling externally.

2. **Practice.** If they were truly honest, most salespeople would admit that they expend a pathetically low amount of energy practicing for early stage sales calls or even for later stage presentations. It's a pretty sad commentary that sellers admit that the majority of the time, they are just winging it. Unlike professional athletes who spend hours laboring on practice fields, driving ranges, free throw lines, and batting cages, most salespeople don't practice at all, and the ones that do, skimp. Not so for Ron. Not only does he insist that the entire team presenting to the prospect must meet to rehearse the day prior to the big meeting, they practice everything, even how they will introduce themselves. Just for grins, how do Ron's requirements for practicing before a big meeting compare to yours? What minimum standards are in place to ensure you (and/or your colleagues) are truly ready for your precious moment in the spotlight? Who is coaching the difficult engineer or the sales support specialist on what not to say? Whether it's how you share the agenda and introduce team members, or how you are going to highlight key differentiators that set your company apart without sounding like you are belittling your competitors, where and how are you practicing and who is providing feedback and coaching? Some may consider Ron obsessive in his standard for prepping and practicing, but no one ever complains about his win-rate against his fiercest competitors.

3. **Personal.** Ron makes his selling personal and he takes it personally too. Along with his taskmaster reputation for getting his side ready to host customer visits or deliver big presentations, he is probably best known for this sales theory: Connection trumps Content. While everyone else is running around arguing about the language in one bullet point or trying to perfect a slide deck, Ron is constantly reminding himself and others that sales is personal and that people make buying decisions for personal reasons. That is part of the reason he has his team work so hard on how to personalize their introductions when kicking off a meeting. Right from the outset, he is looking to establish personal connections between his team members and the prospect's team members. It's also why, at times, Ron asks unusual questions early on during what is supposed to be a presentation. "When you looked at your calendar this morning and saw the two hours blocked with our firm, what were your first thoughts about this meeting and us?" Ron gets prospects to talk because he asks interesting, different questions that others typically are afraid to, and he learns valuable things key people are thinking and feeling that his competitors don't.

4. **Follow-Up.** Rather than share general ways Ron follows up with his prospects, this story about how he successfully helped me to follow up with one of mine is even more valuable. Fifteen years ago, I was working for a great company and trying to close one of the largest deals of my career. Everything had gone really well throughout the entire twelve-month sales cycle, and we were pretty much down to waiting for a decision. It was killing me that I couldn't figure out what else I could do

to increase our odds of winning, and I was sensitive about doing too much follow-up with my key contact at the account. There was also this nagging feeling I had a hard time articulating—I just had the sense that there was something in our final proposal that the prospect didn't love. I finally came to my senses and called Ron. It took me ten minutes to share the backstory on this massive opportunity, and then Ron asked a half-dozen questions to get a feel for where the deal stood. He paused for what felt like eternity but was likely only five seconds.

He audibly exhaled, sounding troubled, and said: "Mike, this doesn't feel right. Your gut is telling you something, and based on everything you shared, I just think you have more selling to do here. You need to follow up without coming across like an impatient, immature salesperson, and you must offer value to the prospect while doing it. Call your contact; you know she likes you. Tell her that you have the sense that they don't have all the critical information necessary to make the best decision. Then ask her what she sees as the Achilles' heel in your proposal. Just ask her flat out what she perceives as the weakness in what was proposed so you can clarify it or provide additional information." I took Ron's advice and called my contact. She thanked me profusely for asking the question and then spelled out exactly what her side's biggest concern was with my company's approach. It probably would have killed the deal if unaddressed. We scheduled another meeting with the prospect's key people and adapted our approach to address their concerns. We were awarded the contract, and I realized right then that Ron might be the very best salesperson I knew.

Sales Friends, I grant you that Tom and Ron are exceptional sellers who have produced extraordinary results for a very long time. They truly are two of the very best salespeople I've ever seen, and my hope is that as you read their stories you were also inspired that their best practices, for the most part, are not extraordinary. Aside from each one's natural sales instincts, which are uniquely theirs, there is nothing they do on a day-to-day basis that you could not do. There is nothing magical or mysterious about how they go about their jobs. Both of these men became top-producing sales professionals through tremendous effort; they had to work at it, and they worked hard to master the fundamentals of selling. As you can see, both still work very hard.

Be encouraged that there is no secret sauce you're missing. Neither Tom nor Ron would tell you that their success came easily, and I know for certain that neither took shortcuts or think they've cracked the "secret sales code." And that is part of the reason I went so hard after the charlatans and false sales teachers in part I of this book. I know we all wish there were shortcuts to sales success, but there are not. Be wary, my friends. Be very wary. Follow the examples of the highly successful sellers I've shared here in part II, and run away as fast as you can from the peddlers who promise you they've got exactly the thing you need to become a sales superstar.

CHAPTER 16

Beyond All Else, Great Sales Leadership Is Still the Key to Winning More New Sales

If I've learned anything from my dozen years going into companies as an outsider to help improve sales performance it is that sales leadership is the absolute key. Salespeople can implement all of the best practices for winning more New Sales described in part II, but if there isn't a healthy, high-performance sales culture, if managers don't hold people accountable for hitting goals and maintaining a robust pipeline of opportunities, and if talent is not managed appropriately where the right people are in the right roles, top producers are retained and underperformance is quickly addressed, then it's all for naught. Sales leadership is crucially important, and no amount of sales skills, sales process, or sales tools will overcome the damage created by poor sales management or an unhealthy sales culture.

That is precisely why I wrote my sales management book and have dedicated more time in the past few years to helping businesses increase sales leadership effectiveness than I have directly coaching and training salespeople. The harsh #SalesTruth is that if companies desire and demand more New Sales, then the first thing management should do is look in the mirror before being so quick to point the finger and declare what the sales force could be doing better!

This past year felt like one giant *Sales Management. Simplified.* World Tour. I was asked to lead workshops for business owners, senior executives, sales leaders, and sales managers on five continents. The single most intriguing takeaway from spending so much time with executives and sales managers from around the globe is that the issues facing all these leaders are not similar; they are identical! Whether I was in St. Louis or San Diego, Spain or South Africa, Singapore or Sao Paulo, the challenges facing sales management were exactly the same, and the solutions to those challenges easy to identify.

Accountability Is Not a Dirty Word

It is really trendy today to talk about the importance of coaching salespeople. And I agree. Coaching is an important part of the sales leader's job. I'm a *huge* fan of managers coaching and mentoring sellers. Throughout my career, I have benefitted tremendously from being coached and mentored by my bosses and absolutely believe managers should be coaching their people whether it's pertaining to sales skills development or strategy for advancing opportunities. Coaching is great. No argument here.

It is even more trendy for leaders to wax eloquently about how they are "enabling" their sales teams and you'd think bonuses were paid every time a confused executive or manager uttered the phrase "sales enablement." I can't make a specific argument against enabling sellers except to mention that I'm not sure you can find three people to agree on what the heck that means.

So while the popular kids are promoting enablement and

praising those who prioritize coaching over managing, I will just offer this little anecdote after spending a ridiculous amount of time observing high and low performing sales leaders: Accountability, particularly when executed well, trumps coaching and enabling every day of the month and twice on the day that the sales report gets published! There is nothing dirty, politically incorrect, or demotivating when managers review a salesperson's actual results against goal and examine the health of that seller's pipeline.

Chapter 20 is the most popular chapter in *Sales Management. Simplified.* and I have seen sales teams' cultures and results transformed simply from managers implementing the best practice outlined for conducting effective one-to-one monthly accountability meetings. Something wonderful and powerful transpires when managers review a salesperson's results, pipeline, and activity against named target accounts (in that specific order).

The very simple act of the sales manager sitting down formally with each salesperson every month—not for coaching, not to listen to excuses, not for reps to ask the manager to do their job, but for the singular purpose of forcing salespeople to answer for what they produced (results), what they are working on to produce results in the future (pipeline), and where they focused (activity) to generate and advance opportunities, is transformative. No tool, no trick, and no training will produce the kind of sales lift created by managers effectively doing their most important job—holding sellers accountable for doing their job. And the beauty of doing accountability well is that it doesn't demotivate team members. Every seller understands that sales is about results and that results are a product of pipeline health (opportunity creation and advancement). Taking that a step further, any salesperson that bristles from a manager committed to reviewing results and inquiring about pipeline health is probably in the wrong job. Let's be honest: a salesperson who resists being held accountable for producing results and filling a pipeline is probably not a salesperson that can ever be counted on to bring in new business.

The Right Executives and an Effective Sales Operations Team Can Change the Game

I rarely mention my clients by name simply to protect their identity and confidentiality. However, occasionally, I am engaged by a company that is doing so much right from a sales leadership perspective, and the experience of working alongside their ubertalented executives is so powerful that I can't not mention it. That is the case with one particular company, where I have spent extensive time over the past two years. Teradata has been so public about our relationship and their initiatives, even blogging about what we were doing together, that I would be remiss not to share this experience with you.

Of the several thousand phone calls during my career, very few are memorable, but the call I received from Nate Holiday, global vice president of sales operations at Teradata, is one that I will not soon forget. He explained their mission to create a "sales destination" culture and a major initiative to invest in frontline sales managers across the globe. Then he asked if I would like to help. My immediate response took him by surprise. "Nate, I'm not sure I heard you right. Can you repeat that, please? I think you said that you and Karen Thomas (the executive vice president for the Americas) were committed to making Teradata's sales culture so desirable that it would become a destination sought out by top sales talent, and you are also looking to increase the effectiveness of your frontline sales managers. But I must have misheard you, because no one wants to do that type of hard work. Most executives are looking to check the box on sales training and move on."

Nate chuckled at my sarcasm and assured me that I heard him correctly. He and Karen were indeed on a mission and believed, as I do, that the frontline manager is the key to driving both a healthy culture and increased results.

I could write an entire book about the fun I have had working with Teradata and Nate, describing what his team has accomplished, and what I learned in the process. It was as energizing and educational and challenging as any engagement in my career. I had many enlightening takeaways from working with Nate, other gifted executives, members of his sales ops team, and country leaders and sales managers around the world, but none as significant as the realization of how powerful and effective a well-led sales operations organization could be.

In most organizations I have observed, sales operations is, for the most part, a nonfactor. They are there. They try. They create things and processes and acquire and implement tools for the sales force. They attempt to assist sales executives and increase visibility and accountability for the field. But in general, they don't make much of an impact, and sometimes the impact they do have is negative. Sales ops often creates work for the sales team. Frequently, their "new and improved" processes and sales tools are cumbersome, unhelpful, and rarely provide value to the field. Most people, including me if polled, would cast a no-confidence vote and complain that in many companies, sales ops serves itself and its own purposes, not the sales team.

Not so at Teradata. What I witnessed firsthand there was very different. Nate regularly warned others in the organization about the "corporate tax" that headquarters and sales ops often places on the field. This "tax" resulted when company leadership imposed rules, requests, and processes on the field, with no concern for the hassle created or opportunity cost incurred. Everything Nate championed was run through his ROI filter, and the question was asked, "What 'tax' is this going to put on the people in the field compared to the benefit it will provide?" His stated mission was for sales ops to create more value for the sales team than it extracted. If we were going to ask the sales force to adopt a new tool, then that tool better provide value and help for the user, not just take/gather information that corporate says it needs. As a leader, Nate was committed to increasing both sales effectiveness and sellers' face time with customers and reducing the corporate tax rate and internal requests that only seemed to serve the corporate machine. Can I get a loud "amen" from the salespeople reading this? Three cheers for a sales ops leader who actually understands that the role is to serve and to support the sales force, not to torture it. Oh, how I wish others would take heed and follow this example.

Even more impressive than Teradata's philosophies regarding sales ops's role was its resolve to invest in sales managers. More than any company with which I've worked, Karen, Nate, and other executives continually demonstrated a commitment to increasing the effectiveness of those leading sales teams in the field. Whether it was having me create workshop sessions to help overburdened managers break their tendency to operate in "Hero Mode" (and refocus time and energy toward making heroes of their salespeople instead of trying to do everyone's job), or the painstaking effort Nate led to make the implementation of Salesforce .com manager-friendly, the commitment was obvious.

I see a lot of less-than-ideal implementations of Salesforce.com and am the first one to offer stern warnings to sales leaders that as wonderful a tool as SFDC may be, it will not fix your sales, sales process, and sales management issues by itself. The sales ops team at Teradata went to extreme lengths to not only customize

Salesforce to the *n*th degree, but to create beautiful and useful manager dashboards built around the *Sales Management. Simplified.* accountability and coaching frameworks we were teaching in workshops. I have never seen a better aligned, more customized, or more rapidly adopted implementation of SFDC. Huge props to Nate and company for an unwavering resolve not to settle but to do this right.

Following the rollout, they invested in an additional round of customized workshops where we had managers practice conducting accountability and coaching sessions using Teradata's new dashboards, and the feedback from managers was outstanding. They truly appreciated the company's commitment to helping them succeed.

My biggest takeaway from this engagement and strongest exhortation to senior executives is that it truly matters who is leading your sales operations initiative. Nate and I had extensive conversations about this and are in agreement that the success of his sales ops team and these major initiatives were due, in large part, to the fact that prior to taking on this role, he was a highly successful salesperson for the company. He came from the field! I believe that the only way to get this kind of lift (and respect) when looking to stand up a sales operations team is to put a top producer in the leadership role. Not an administrator. Not a struggling salesperson for whom you're looking to provide a soft landing and safe haven. You need a proven high performer who understands exactly what the field needs to win and garners immediate respect because of that person's past success. From the moment Nate stepped into his executive position leading sales operations, his overriding passion was to support the field. His self-proclaimed mission was to win over hearts internally to think "field first." I can attest that his mission was accomplished, and the company's pipeline health and results prove it.

It's Very Hard to Win New Sales Without the Right People in the Right Roles

I admit it. When it comes to the topic of sales talent, I sound like a broken record playing the same song over and over and over. I am not sorry about repeating myself. Everywhere I turn, this is an issue! Just yesterday sitting with the leadership team at our marketing agency, unsolicited, an executive shared her frustration with companies that continued asking "farmer" salespeople to hunt for new business. I nodded in vehement agreement and shared that I actually refer to that type of salesperson as a "zookeeper." These wonderful, service-oriented, account-management-focused sellers are masters at *caring* for their existing customers. They feed them, protect them, bathe and groom them. These zookeepers are awesome at serving, keeping, and renewing current customers, but are typically not very useful for proactively acquiring new pieces of business.

My confusion results from the fact that no one argues with me when I compare and contrast sales hunters and zookeepers. There is pretty much universal agreement that most hunters don't excel at managing the day-to-day needs of existing customers, and that there is an enormous opportunity cost from tasking the precious few true hunters on your team with the heavy service burden of managing accounts. Similarly, there is nary a disagreement when I question management's sanity for continuing to irrationally hope that their vegetarian, peacekeeping, conflict-averse, relationship-first zookeepers will turn into spear-throwing, bloodthirsty big game hunting, successful new business developers.

Different strokes for different folks, but why are most executives so unwilling to tackle this topic head-on and do the hard work to further define sales roles? I shake my head because, while

I rarely hear counterarguments to my oversimplified hunter-zoo-keeper theory, it is even more rare to find sales leaders expending the effort to actually create more specific roles and then put the right people in those roles.

Further compounding underperformance caused by hiring sales talent misaligned with requirements of the job are the human resources people inserting their biases into the equation. I used to be amused hearing HR managers preach about the importance of hiring collaborative team players for sales roles. Today, however, I am more angry than amused, because I've seen the resulting damage firsthand. The moment I hear this nonsense or read a job description for a sales hunter role that describes the ideal candidate as someone who plays nice with others, I loudly protest and raise the red flag. Are you really looking for people who would consider *collaboration* and playing good corporate citizen the attributes of which they're most proud? Or are you seeking a fearless warrior to send out into the wild to hunt for food that the entire company depends on for sustenance? Yeah, that's what I thought. So, let's think twice before recruiting people wired like peacekeepers for (New Sales) positions that require a killer mentality to succeed.

I am so serious about protecting clients from making bad hires that I've begun pushing sales leaders to redo job postings for sales positions. Instead of including all the typical, flowery, boilerplate language about the company and the role, just tell the truth about the job and who will succeed in it. Write the job description to repel the wrong candidates and attract the right ones!

The very best example of this is the story about Rock Star back in chapter 13. We knew exactly who we needed to thrive in this role. My client was seeking a driven, fearless, new-business developer who could both self-generate new opportunities and then go toe-to-toe with senior executives in a boardroom. When we wrote the job description for the search firm, along with all the attractive elements of the role, we made it abundantly clear that the ideal candidate would . . .

- Believe that traditional prospecting was still effective for securing meetings
- Understand that while the company did attend trade shows, speak at industry events, and receive regular inbound inquiries, the salesperson would be responsible for self-generating more than 50 percent of new sales opportunities
- Be very comfortable picking up the phone

The job ad also contained language dissuading candidates from applying if they were not open to being held accountable for filling the pipeline via their own personal sales efforts. The result was wonderful. The ad scared off the poseurs and attracted the type of candidates we were seeking, including Rock Star, who is the single best hire I've seen a company make.

Management need not live perpetually frustrated that their account management-wired salespeople struggle bringing in new business because they either cannot or will not hunt. That's how zookeepers behave; it's who they are. Imagine what might happen to your team's overall performance if you further defined the sales roles so people could thrive operating virtually stress free in their areas of natural giftedness. How much fun would it be and how many more New Sales would be generated if you put true hunters in hunting roles and zookeepers/farmers in account management roles? This I can promise: Everyone would be happier—the customers, the salespeople, and sales management, and sales would increase dramatically.

Implement These Two Iron Laws of Recruiting

Recruiting does not happen by accident. Most sales managers work too many hours, receive too many emails, get dragged into too many meetings, and have way too much on their plate. Due to this overload, which nonurgent task do you think often gets ignored? Recruiting.

The paradox here is that possibly the single most important job of the sales leader is to staff the team with the best fit and highest quality talent available. Yet, recruiting is typically the first responsibility to get shelved simply because it's not urgent, and it is very rare that managers are held accountable for their recruiting efforts unless they're currently understaffed.

I have two Iron Laws when it comes to recruiting sales talent:

1. **Recruit ahead of the need.** It is a whole lot easier to add solid talent to your team when you already have a "bench" of potential new hires selected. That is exactly why it is imperative for managers to regularly carve out dedicated chunks of calendar time to recruit. In the past year, a handful of sales managers in different industries have confessed to me that they held off having hard conversations with underperforming salespeople, because they were afraid the salespeople might feel threatened and look to leave. If that doesn't sit right with you, welcome to the club. These weak managers told me straight out that they didn't want the hassle of either having to deal with an empty territory or the grief of recruiting a replacement for the underperformer. Friends, I cannot say this any plainer or any stronger: That is management malpractice! Ignoring underperformance because you are afraid of the consequences of addressing it or are too

lazy to do the important work of finding the right candidate demonstrates both incompetence and indifference. Carving out just a few hours per month to build a bench of potential candidates is the best practice that prevents managers from getting in that unenviable position where they feel trapped and are unwilling to hold people accountable.

2. **Never hire a candidate who is not better than the average person on your team.** If the candidate doesn't raise the bar, then walk away. The moment you hire someone who brings down your average, you have put yourself and your team on a very dangerous slippery slope. When you settle by adding someone to your team that everyone realizes is not up to par, it sends an awful message and has the potential of destroying your culture. One of my mentors, David Kuenzle, who was mentioned in the earlier discussion about being wary of looking at averages, has a very powerful quote when it comes to assessing talent. David would challenge managers to consider that "no breath is often better than bad breath." I like that expression for several reasons, particularly when it comes to managing sales talent. I have seen this, and I am sure many of you have too. Often, that warm body we keep in the job does more damage to our company and the business than if, temporarily, there was nobody in the role.

I can only fantasize about the potential increase in sales if companies were to truly hold salespeople accountable for results and pipeline health, were conscious of the corporate tax put on sales teams, equipped sellers and managers with tools that actually increased productivity, and if true sales hunters were better supported and freed up to hunt, while zookeepers were simply charged with caring for accounts entrusted to them, all while sales leaders prioritized managing talent and recruiting to get the best people in the best-fit roles.

CHAPTER 17

Stop Searching for the Secret Sales Sauce, Ignore the Trendy Voices, and Get to Work Mastering the Fundamentals

My sincere hope as we wrap up our #SalesTruth journey is that despite all the noise and nonsense, one of your big takeaways is that there really is not much new under the sun when it comes to professional selling and sales management. Oh, there are (thousands of) sales tool vendors and supposed thought leaders who will scoff at that assessment and vehemently disagree, but what I have observed across various continents, industries, companies, and sales roles screams otherwise.

Be wary of the online "experts" who are all too quick to proclaim that *everything* about sales and selling has changed. Be even more wary when they poke fun at those who are succeeding using proven, tried, and true methods. And be downright skeptical when these "experts" point to the popularity of their LinkedIn posts as evidence that their theories and advice are credible.

Just this morning, as I was preparing to write this final chapter, Anthony Iannarino pointed to an online article in *Inc.* magazine posted by a columnist and supposed sales guru. The piece is titled

"It's Official: Cold-Calling Is Dead and Buried," and the writer made the case that technology has rendered calling prospects by phone moot. It's a well-written piece, and I'm sure it communicates exactly what many in sales want to hear. But there's just one little problem: It's not true. In fact, the claims made in the article, while popular, are blatantly false.

I was just in Birmingham where I had been invited back to deliver the keynote for a large company's sales kickoff meeting for the second year in a row. When I finished speaking, several sales reps lined up to chat with me. Two of them shared that they were coming off record years and thanked me for my message the prior year when I challenged them to carve out more time for prospecting. They credited their increased results specifically to the fact that they committed more time and energy to prospecting instead of relying on leads from the company and hoping that overservicing their existing accounts would drive new business.

Last week on LinkedIn, Miles Veth, a young, up-and-coming star in the sales-improvement business, posted actual results that his outsourced prospecting firm had achieved for several clients. The numbers were staggering. His little team of prospectors was securing meetings with high-level contacts at his clients' dream target accounts. Miles even posted the number of outbound calls his people were making, along with the number of voicemails left, live conversations conducted, and appointments secured. The only reason I share this so specifically is because, all too often, articles like the one in *Inc.* go unchallenged. People read the nonsense about prospecting and the phone being dead and assume that because it's published it is true. It's time to wake up, people! Access to a keyboard and a web site, even one with a supposedly trustworthy brand name, does not a valid sales expert make. Whether it's the confused #socialselling promoter twisting himself in knots trying to convince you that Kylie Jenner posting selfies is your role model to become a top B2B sales professional (see chapter 2), or this "columnist" for *Inc.* incorrectly claiming that the phone is as useless as your appendix, stop believing the nonsense in search of the new secret sales sauce!

If you are looking to achieve breakthrough sales success, the single most important thing you can do is dedicate yourself to becoming a master at creating your own new sales opportunities. Everywhere I look, there is an overabundance of salespeople *chasing* opportunities, but very few laser-focused on *creating* opportunities, and even fewer who have mastered this critical skill. The formula to do so is not hard. In fact, it's rather simple as outlined in chapters 7 through 11. You must adopt the right mindset about developing new business and believe that you have the power and ability to self-generate opportunities. And that ability only increases when your motivation is pure and you believe, beyond a shadow of a doubt, that you not only deliver great value to your customers, but that they will be better off and experience better outcomes by working with you.

Belief, however, is not enough to *create* sales opportunities; you must commit more of your calendar to allow sufficient time for proactively pursuing strategic target accounts. Playing glorified customer service rep and over-allocating time to your favorite, but not growable, accounts will not fill your pipeline with more opportunities. Get a firm grasp on your highest-value, highest-payoff new-business-development activities and block chunks of calendar time exclusively for those activities. Get over your addiction to your email inbox and stop telling customers to call you whenever they need something. Become more *selfishly productive* to allow yourself to spend more time doing the precious few activities that truly move the needle when it comes to opportunity creation. I cannot stress this enough: Top producers consistently bring in more new business because they have become really, really good at not allowing others to put work on their plates. They are selfish—in a good way—and maximize selling time spent working to create, advance, and close opportunities. Period.

Put in the effort to sharpen your messaging. Nothing will increase your confidence or make you more effective and comfortable pursuing new opportunities than a compelling, customer-issue, and outcome-focused message. Avoid the commodity trap that results from making your offerings the focus of your sales story, and resist the temptation to lead into your message by bragging about how great and different your company or solution is. Deploy the foolproof method offered in chapter 10 to *bridge* into the issues your solution addresses and the outcomes it produces. I promise that the entire dynamic surrounding prospecting changes when your messaging is focused on what's in it for the prospect. For further reading on sharpening your sales story, see chapters 7 and 8 in *New Sales. Simplified.*

Use every ethical and effective means necessary—yes, including the good old-fashioned telephone—to secure early stage meetings with prospective customers. Don't make the proactive prospecting call into something bigger, scarier, and more daunting than it is. *You* are a professional representing a business that likely has a better solution, and you are pursuing a conversation with someone who likely has a need. Make the call. Sound normal. Acknowledge that you are interrupting. Share a value nugget or two about the types of issues you address (or outcomes your solution achieves) and ask the prospect to meet with you. Expect resistance and be prepared to ask a few more times for the meeting, all the while promising value, ideas, and insight to the prospect regardless of whether there is a next step for you. And accept the reality that voicemail and gatekeepers are part of life in sales, so instead of dreading them, view both voicemail and gatekeepers as part of your sales arsenal and use them to deliver your message. Above all else, keep in mind that prospecting is a game. "No" is not a personal rejection, and it typically takes multiple asks to secure a meeting and multiple voice messages to earn a return call. Play the game and play it well. The better you get at the game, the more fun you will have and the more meetings with strategic target prospects you will secure.

Once you create a new early-stage opportunity, please remember that in just about every situation, discovery should precede presentation. Stop rushing to demo your product/software or conduct a presentation. There is no way to be perceived as a true professional problem solver, consultant, or value-creator when you show up in pitch mode before doing solid discovery work. And once you have created a real opportunity and are working to advance it, get as close as you can to the businesspeople who care about the value your solution will create. The key to staying out of the procurement pit is to convince the key stakeholders that you and your solution will produce the absolute best outcome for them. When you do that well, you put yourself in the best possible position to follow your own sales process, as opposed to the customer's procurement people dictating what they want you to do. If you have a hard time believing that you don't have to be a victim of your giant customer's purchasing or supply-chain management department, go back and reread the success stories of those small companies in chapter 13. In all of those cases, the little *David* decided not to acquiesce to the giant *Goliath*'s procurement process and instead won really big, really important deals by sticking to his guns.

Please remember that if you think you need the very best product or the lowest price to succeed in sales, then you will never succeed without them. Frankly, if you're selling a superior product or have the best price, you probably are not necessary in the equation. So, I'd suggest being very, very slow to whine about having to sell less than perfect products or at higher prices.

The very highest producing salespeople I have observed are not freaks of nature. They don't deploy extreme techniques, and they rarely, if ever, talk about sales tools or what new tricks they're using. Similar to Ron and Tom in chapter 15, the salespeople I see crushing it year after year are the ones who have absolutely mastered the fundamentals of selling. I wish there were secrets to share, but the #SalesTruth is that there aren't. So, my strongest encouragement is stop looking for shortcuts or the secret sales sauce. Do. The. Work. Master the basics.

If you would like to keep up with me, you can do so on Twitter and Instagram following @mike_weinberg, and I blog at mikeweinberg.com. I wish you tremendous success, many New Sales, and great sales leadership!

Index

INDEX